{PRAISE FOR}

SADDLED

"Raw and poignant . . . With a writing style so clean and honest, it's easy to imagine Susan is your best friend from college or your beloved next-door neighbor . . . You will root for her to find the direction and control she needs to be that strong person not only for Georgia's sake, but for herself. She does not disappoint."

—*Boston Examiner*

"Animal lovers and recovering alcoholics will be inspired by this story."

—*Library Journal*

"Reading this book was like having an unflinchingly honest talk with a close friend about her struggle for meaning and hope after a devastating relationship and descent into alcoholism. It took a horse to give Susan the strength to change."

—Stacey O'Brien, author of *Wesley the Owl*

"Can a book be both looking glass and richly colored animal portrait? In *Saddled,* Susan Richards performs dual literary magic by giving us the history of a horse-woman retrieving her life from the bottom of the wine glass, and a mirror in which the sensitive reader will see herself again and again. I loved every sentence in this superlative memoir."

— Melissa Pierson, author of
Dark Horses and Black Beauties

"Susan Richards masterfully weaves together her compelling story of life lived on the edge with vivid accounts of a horse who gives her reasons to live and ultimately to thrive. Horse lovers will relate to their healing connection; people who know little about horses will be amazed at the benefits that occur when a horse and human forge bonds of unfailing trust and loyalty."

—Allen and Linda Anderson, founders of the
Angel Animals Network and authors of
Horses with a Mission and *Angel Horses*

"*Chosen by a Horse* contained hints of a childhood among wicked adults; *Saddled* fills in the details. When Susan Richards needed one sane place to stand against the stresses of a crazy world, her Morgan horse, Georgia, was there to show her that loving an animal grounds you in a way that nothing else can."

—Sharon Sakson, author of *Paws & Effect:
The Healing Power of Dogs*

"Saddle up and enjoy the ride with Susan Richards.
You'll love it."
—Rita Mae Brown

CHOSEN BY A HORSE

"This is an inspirational story of what family means,
and what the loss of one can do to us, and for us."
—*Boston Globe*

"Two kindred spirits find each other in this beautifully
written memoir about the human-animal bond."
—Temple Grandin, author of
Animals Make Us Human

"An incredibly moving story, beautifully written
and insightful."
—*Roanoke Times*

"A tender lesson in courage and dependence."
—*Kirkus Reviews*

BOOKS BY SUSAN RICHARDS

Chosen by a Horse

Chosen Forever

Saddled

SADDLED

How a Spirited Horse
Reined Me In and Set Me Free

Susan Richards

MARINER BOOKS
HOUGHTON MIFFLIN HARCOURT · *Boston* · *New York*

First Mariner Books edition 2011

www.hmhbooks.com

Library of Congress Cataloging-in-Publication Data
Richards, Susan, date.
    Saddled : how a spirited horse reined me in and set me free / Susan Richards.
        p. cm.
    ISBN 978-0-547-24172-2   ISBN 978-0-547-37629-5 (pbk.)
        1. Horses — New York (State) — Anecdotes.   2. Richards, Susan, date.
    3. Women horse owners — New York (State) — Anecdotes.   4. Human-animal
    relationships — New York (State) — Anecdotes.   I. Title.
    SF301.R528 2010
    636.1092—dc22
    [B]   2009047468

The names of the some of the people mentioned in this book have been changed.

Book design by Lisa Diercks
The text of this book is set in Dante.

Printed in the United States of America
DOC 10 9 8 7 6 5 4 3 2 1

To Lloyd, who shared the best and the worst of the ride

SADDLED

{ CHAPTER 1 }

IT WAS LATE FALL, and my cousin Holly and I were galloping down an old dirt logging road near the Adirondack farm I'd just bought. I was on my new Morgan mare, Georgia, and Holly was on a bay quarter-horse mare named Nikka, who boarded in my barn. The air was sweet with the smell of white pine and horse sweat, and I was laughing even though I was so depressed about a disastrous marriage and a drinking problem that I didn't care if I fell off my horse and died. I always laughed when I galloped a horse. Even when I was so hung over that my hands shook or when the night before was a blur of violent confrontations with my husband.

I'd had Georgia less than a week. That morning she'd kicked our stable help, Alan, out of her stall, slamming him so hard against the wall it had knocked the wind out of him. I'd grabbed her halter and dragged her outside. No, wait. She had dragged me outside, but once there, I'd finally asserted control and punched her on the rear flank, yelling *No!* She had turned to look at me standing next to her rear leg, thinking maybe I was getting ready to slug her again. *Are you crazy?* I shouted into her placid eyes.

How fast a horse blinks can tell you a lot.

At first she didn't blink at all, but when she did, it was so slow I could have recited a short poem by the time the thick-lashed lids ho-hummed their way back open.

Either she didn't feel the punch or she didn't care. Her ears were straight up and perked forward, perhaps listening for the sound of fresh hay being scattered on the ground or just enjoying the full attention of the human at her side, even though the human seemed temporarily demented. We looked at each other for a long time. I glared at her and she? She *bah-linked.*

I was looking for guilt, for some indication that she understood kicking was very, very bad. It would have been OK if she had looked scared, if she had danced away from me, scooting her flank out of reach of the terrible hitting hand. But she hadn't. It wasn't that we didn't understand each other, that we had somehow failed to communicate our point of view. We had. I was sorry that she had kicked Alan, and she wasn't. *Bah-link.*

Later we galloped through the woods on that crisp fall morning, the incident forgotten, while laughter ripped its way through my despair. *My worst fear has come true,* I'd written in my journal earlier that day. *I'm an alcoholic. My life, my marriage — it's all a sham.*

My worst fear had actually come true years before, but it was only that morning that I'd named it for what it was, that I had written it down. *Alcoholic.* It seemed as bad as cancer, maybe worse because this felt like an elective, like one of those classes you took at college just for the fun of it. Something you decided sounded better than the dozens of other classes you could have taken. *Alcoholism,* you might have written on your registration form after reading the course description: *Students will learn to drink large amounts of alcohol, often surreptitiously, while pretending to suffer no ill effects. Prerequisites include the ability to lie and a strong belief that the laws of physics and biochemistry and irrefutable evidence of any kind that attempts to undermine a lifestyle of complete dissipation applies only to others.*

I'd been waking up hung over since 1970. Nine years. It seemed like a long time not to see something as obvious as a drinking problem. But denial was part of the course description, the part where you lied a lot, which included lying to yourself. I was good at that. I was good at all of it. Except suddenly I was almost thirty, and I knew what I hadn't known the day before or the week before or the year before. Why now?

It had something to do with Georgia. It had something to do with making a commitment as enormous as caring for a horse who might live as my companion for the next forty years. It had something to do with love. My search for a horse had lasted almost a year and taken me all over the Northeast — from the best Morgan-breeding farms in Vermont, New Hampshire, and New York to the backyard paddocks in the suburbs of Boston where young girls had gone off to college, leaving their passion for horses behind.

I had known I wanted a Morgan since I was seven years old and had outgrown Bunty, the impossible but beloved Shetland pony my grandmother had given me when I was six. After two years of being bitten, kicked, and thrown, I saw my riding instructor appear at my lesson one day leading a Morgan gelding school-horse for me to ride. I fell in love with Alert's stocky, muscular beauty as he effortlessly carried me around pony-club show rings and later on cross-country hunts and bareback swims in nearby Langley Pond. The breed is known for its endurance and versatility, and there seemed to be nothing Alert wasn't willing to do. His steady good nature and love of being ridden endeared me to the breed forever, and I longed for the day when I could have my own Morgan.

That day came on a late fall afternoon in upstate New York when, to get away from a husband I'd grown to hate, I'd hopped in the car and driven four hours to a well-known Morgan breeder near Syracuse who had lots of stock for sale. I don't know why I thought bringing a horse into the chaos in my life was a good idea. I just knew that for the past year, looking for what I had come to refer to as my Morgan had given me the only peace and sanity I had.

It was as clear and crisp as a fall day can get when I turned off the main road and onto the long dirt drive that led past dozens of Morgans pastured on both sides of the road that cut the farm in half. I drove slowly, letting my eyes wander over the beautiful faces and graceful arched necks for which Morgans are so prized. I was looking for signs of poor health or poor breeding, either of which would have ended my search on the spot, before I'd even met the owner. But I was also looking for something else, not in the herds grazing almost to the horizon on either side of my car, but for something inside myself, a sense of recognition or connection that would let me know when I'd found my horse. In all the horses I'd seen in my year of looking, I'd never once felt this. I'd never felt *That's my horse,* and I knew I wouldn't buy one until I did.

What I didn't realize was that in my search for a horse, I was conducting another search, a much older one connected to my first memories of a horse as a traumatized six-year-old dealing with the death of her mother and the disappearance of her father. Into that gaping void had stepped Bunty, a gift from Grandmother Richards, who must have known she was throwing me a lifeline, the only one she had in her limited ability to nurture but, as it turned out, the best anyone could have offered. My reaction had been immediate and visceral, a heart-pounding recognition that I was in the presence of something wonderful beyond belief, the most spontaneous outpouring of love I had ever felt. In that moment I became someone else, someone who was more than just a girl who'd lost her home and parents. I became a girl who loved that pony. I became a girl who loved horses.

Twenty-four years later, traumatized by a battering husband and a growing sense of shame about my drinking, I was in need of another lifeline. And of all the ways in which I might have searched for help, turning toward horses had been instinctive. I wasn't just looking for *any* love; I was looking for *that* love, that first involuntary spasm that jolted my five-year-old heart back to life at the sight of a Shetland pony named Bunty.

I hadn't expected to find my horse that fall day. As I headed down the dirt drive looking from pasture to pasture, I saw many healthy, well-bred equines, but not one of them "spoke" to me. The drive ended at several large red barns, all in need of repair and fresh paint. Except for the fifty or so horses grazing in various pastures, the place looked deserted. There were empty silos where the roofs had caved in, and the front porch on the main house looked dangerously close to falling off. When I parked and got out of the car, a couple of mangy-looking black dogs had ambled across the barnyard to pee on my tires.

I was debating whether to get back in the car and leave because I hadn't seen "my" horse grazing in any of the pastures, and I didn't want to waste the owner's time in showing me a lot of horses I knew I didn't want, when I turned around and looked up the road I had just driven down. There in the distance, a quarter of a mile away, was a heavy-set man driving a two-wheeled cart being pulled by a chestnut red Morgan. Either the horse didn't like being driven or this was her first day in harness because she yanked the cart from one side of the road to the other, occasionally breaking into a short gallop before the driver was able to pull her back to a trot. She'd settle down for a minute before she'd give a little buck and bolt again. But none of that seemed important compared with the instant certainty I felt that I was watching someone else drive *my* horse. Even from a distance I could tell she wasn't bad, only untrained and giddy on this windy fall day, dancing out her joy in heading back to the barn after an unpleasant lesson in something she didn't yet understand.

By the time the driver pulled her to a fidgety stop near

where I was standing, I felt almost proprietary about her. I reached up with one hand on her bridle to help hold her still while my other hand stroked the thick sweaty neck. Her large almond-shaped eyes didn't show the least bit of interest in me, only a great impatience at wanting to be free of the harness so she could join the herd grazing in the pastures beyond. But I had fallen in love with the bold youngster with the beautiful chiseled red face, and nothing was going to separate us until I knew for sure she was mine.

I spoke briefly to the driver, who was the farm's trainer, and he said this was, indeed, her first day in harness. She was three years old, and in what must have been the understatement of the day, he explained she was still pretty green.

I nodded, laughing. *What's her name?* I asked.

Rockridge Georgiegirl, he said, *but everybody calls her Georgia. She's all heart,* he added, giving her mane an affectionate tug, *and about the most opinionated animal on this farm.*

In horse lingo *heart* means gusto, pizzazz, a willingness to go anywhere and try anything. Not blindly, but with an expansiveness of spirit and intelligence that are visible in a horse's posture and eye. Heart is confidence. It is the biggest difference between a good horse and an extraordinary one, and Georgia had heart. I could see it the minute she appeared on the horizon pulling the cart, the way she cocked her head and carried her tail stiff and high, the way she *laughed* with her whole body as she tangoed down that road. She was audacious, too, bold enough to defy her trainer. *Opinionated,* he called it. Well, why not? Who didn't have an opinion? But in a world run by humans, only a confident horse would dare express it. I liked her trainer. It meant he hadn't been too heavy-handed with her. He hadn't forced his diva into the chorus line.

In a few minutes the owner of the farm appeared, a thin, tired-looking woman dressed in jeans and smoking a cigarette. We had spoken on the phone earlier in the week, and she had given me some background on the various horses she had for sale.

She's not one of 'em, she said, flicking her ash in the direction of Georgia. *She's too green and too much of a hothead*, she added.

I barely heard her, or, rather, I barely listened because it didn't matter what she said. I knew I'd found my horse. As the woman moved away from Georgia in the direction of the horses that were for sale, I didn't follow her. I stayed next to Georgia, holding the head that didn't want to be still, until the woman stopped and turned around, aware that I wasn't behind her. She looked at me for a minute and then she knew. The trainer knew, and I think even Georgia knew — we all knew that this horse belonged with me. The owner made a halfhearted attempt to talk me out of it, and when she saw she couldn't, she offered to keep Georgia for a few more months to let the trainer work out the "bugs." But in my mind, the only bugs to work out were how much she wanted for the horse and how we were going to get her back to my farm. Both were settled quickly, and the very next day Georgia arrived in Lake Placid.

As soon as I had found Georgia, as soon as I saw her and experienced that spontaneous outpouring of love, I knew I had been altered irrevocably. It's impossible to open your heart that wide and not be changed in the process. I wanted to protect that love, and I couldn't do it by lying to myself, not about drinking or anything else. I'd had her less than a week, but already she was working her magic. I was no longer just a woman in a bad marriage who drank too much. I was the woman who loved Georgia.

A few days after Georgia's arrival, my cousin came to visit and we went riding. I could hear Holly's laughter and Nikka's hoofbeat behind me on the trail. Nikka was the perfect companion horse. Dependable, good-natured, smooth gaited, and willing to let Georgia rule the barn. Nikka had been there first, a loan from a young woman who had recently left for college. The day Georgia arrived after her long trip to my farm, she stepped off the trailer and went right after Nikka, who was standing nearby with her head up and her ears forward, ready with a friendly greeting for her new pasture mate. At the last minute Georgia changed her mind, and instead of sinking her teeth into Nikka, she spun around and kicked hard, sending Nikka fleeing across the field. *What have I done?* I thought. Georgia's previous owner and I watched at the fence as a squealing Georgia chased Nikka around the five-acre field.

She's got a lot of heart, chuckled her former owner, flicking the ash from her cigarette.

That's heart?

Completely ignored in this pasture drama was a third horse, an old Welsh pony named Thunder, a retiree from a nearby amusement park, who trotted behind Georgia trying to get a sniff of the red diva who had suddenly appeared. Georgia seemed to have no issue with him whatsoever, and when it became obvious that Nikka was not going to challenge her alpha status, she dropped her grudge against Nikka as well, and the chase ended as quickly as it had begun. Within hours they were a cohesive herd, dominated by the three-year-old arrival. The three grazed quietly, crowded together in the middle of the pasture as if the other four and three-quarter acres didn't exist.

As Holly and I galloped down the dirt road, I kept a loose rein on Georgia, letting her determine how fast she wanted to go. As long as the road was straight and flat, I enjoyed letting her set the pace; because much about her was still new to me, I was curious to see how she would behave with a free rein. She always began with a buck but settled down quickly, stretching into a smooth, powerful canter, slowly easing herself into a gallop as she realized I wasn't going to stop her.

There is something intensely solitary about galloping on horseback, as though horse and rider become a single unit, shooting through space with just the smell of pine to hint that they are still earthbound. Perhaps it is nothing more than excess adrenaline that makes the experience so isolating, but perhaps it is something else, something darker that explains the feeling of being locked inside a speeding cocoon hurtling toward oblivion. Maybe it was because of all the things that made me drink, all the ways in which I felt inadequate and unfit for the "job," any job, particularly for the job of living. Maybe it was because I had no answers, and with no answers you get no meaning, so oblivion is the only place left to go.

Something golden with flying flaxen hair broke into our cocoon, brushing my leg as it galloped ahead of us. It was Thunder, loose on the trail and free to follow us like a dog. He'd stop to nibble green delicacies along the way, and when we'd get too far ahead, he'd run to catch up, bucking his joy at Georgia as he charged past her. Sometimes my one-year-old dog, a Newfoundland named Bear, would be right behind him, and we'd watch the two of them disappear ahead of us down the trail. It was a funny sight, this odd pair flying through the trees, two creatures who by nature moved as little as possible. Georgia no longer seemed to mind not being the leader and slowed her pace to allow them to pass. The logging roads zigzagged for miles through these woods, and even after cross-country skiing on them all winter and riding on them all summer, I never ran out of new roads to try. Sometimes Thunder would stop at an intersection and wait for us, and sometimes he wouldn't. But it never took him long to discover if we'd taken a different way, and soon enough we'd see that flash of gold beside us as he charged ahead.

We'd been riding for about two hours when I saw light through the trees ahead of us. I rose slightly out of the saddle and pulled back gently on the reins. *Whoa, girl,* I said to Georgia and watched her ears flicker in response to my voice. I liked that she listened to me. I always reinforced any leg or hand signals I gave her with my voice so she would be completely voice trained one day. She slowed reluctantly, a three-year-old with enormous stamina, seemingly happy to run all day. But I didn't know what the light ahead indicated. A clearing full of tree stumps? A pond? A river? It was better to slow down than to discover too late it was a gravel pit or some other landscape that could injure a running horse.

We slowed gradually, and Holly pulled up beside me on Nikka, both horses breathing hard as we trotted out of the woods into a large mowed field. Thunder was already grazing and Bear lay nearby panting. It was a beautiful field, about ten acres surrounded on all sides by pine forests and distant mountains. At the far end was a small log house, and near that, at the edge of the field parked along the tree line, were four small airplanes. We had ridden onto someone's private airstrip. Concerned about the horses' tearing up the perfect grass, we kept to the edge of the field as we rode toward the house to see if we could meet the owner. As the crow flies, he was sort of a neighbor, two hours by horseback and who knew how far by car. I wasn't even sure in what direction we had ridden.

Before we'd ridden halfway to the house, we saw a man emerge from a back door and begin walking across the field toward us. I had trespassed accidentally before on other properties but had never had a bad experience introducing myself to the landowner and apologizing for the intrusion. I had made several new friends that way, and judging from the expression on this man's face as he came closer, it was very likely I would be making another. He was a handsome man with thick brown wavy hair, a muscular build, and a big smile directed straight at Holly.

How ya doin'? he said, coming to a stop between the two horses but reaching his hand out to stroke Nikka's sweaty neck while grinning up at Holly. *I'm Mike.*

Holly grinned back, tossing her shoulder-length brown hair out of her eyes. *Holly,* she said, almost giggling.

They'd known each other less than thirty seconds and already they were flirting, their chemistry so palpable it was like walking into a warm rain.

We're neighbors, I said, waving my hand back toward the woods, *somewhere over there.*

I know where you live, he said. *I've seen these two in your pasture.* He nodded toward Nikka and Thunder.

Our horses danced impatiently on either side of him, pulling downward on the reins toward the grass. I let my reins fall onto Georgia's neck, and she stopped dancing and lowered her head to graze. Holly did the same thing on Nikka, and for a moment it was wonderfully quiet except for the rhythmic sound of ripping grass and the dull grinding of teeth.

I don't remember what we talked about in the next few minutes. I just had the sense that something exciting was happening right in front my eyes. Holly and I had grown up together and talked about everything under the sun including, recently, men, and how she might one day meet the right man despite many false starts. At twenty-five, she was six years younger than I and in no rush to marry. Still, she was ready to meet someone special.

We learned Mike was an artist (so was Holly) who taught painting at a local art school. We learned he lived here full-time and collected and flew antique planes. And after asking, we learned it was OK to ride down his runway if we stayed to the side so we wouldn't rip up the sod down the middle.

Drop by anytime, I called over my shoulder as we took off toward the tree line. Cantering through the woods on a dirt trail is a heady experience, but cantering across a wide-open meadow is even better. Open space is intoxicating to a horse, and all three of them raced down that runway bucking and snorting like a herd of wild mustangs.

Hours later Holly and I sat in rocking chairs in my newl built sunroom off the kitchen, watching the horses graz in the pasture down the hill below us. We sipped mu of tea and rehashed the day's ride, including the irony bumping into an attractive single man in the middle nowhere. It was hard enough to meet a man in Bost where Holly worked as a counselor in a group home, but stumbling on one in the woods? We shared our incredulity in hushed voices, careful not to disturb my husband, who was in an upstairs bedroom recovering from a heart attack.

My life was a crazy mix of good and bad, of luck and misfortune, of hope and despair: this beautiful farm, the horses below us in the pasture, even the kitchen behind me, just renovated with a Mexican tile floor, complete with the dog prints left in by a contractor who knew I would like them. But I was in a loveless marriage and drinking myself to death. I had dreamed of living in the Adirondacks since I was a child. And here I was, almost thirty-one, the dream both realized and ruined.

I didn't want tea. I wanted a glass of white wine, but embarrassment kept me from pouring one in front of Holly until at least five o'clock. I'd been wanting a drink all day, but I forced myself to wait, the last remnant of control in a battle I knew I'd lost. Fear gripped me when I remembered the journal entry from that morning. What did it mean? What would happen to me now? Even as I laughed with Holly about our exhilarating ride, even as I watched my beloved new horse content in her alpine meadow with views of the high peaks beyond, even surrounded by all the trappings of a charmed life, I wondered if I had the courage to kill myself. I couldn't stop drinking and I couldn't live with the shame.

What about my marriage? It was less than a year old and a complete failure, partly because of the reckless decision-making that comes with alcoholism and partly the result of a fatal neediness I was too proud to acknowledge, even to myself. I'd married a man I hardly knew, a man who drank more than I did, which made it easier to deny my own problem. I lived in Boston and he lived near Lake Placid. After visiting him there for the first time, it was the memory of the farm he rented — one hundred acres in the middle of the Adirondack State Park, with pastures for horses and views of the high peaks — that had lingered in my imagination. I had gone to camp in the Adirondacks for nine straight summers — the happiest days of my childhood — where I had established a deep love for the area. As an adult, I had been living in and around Boston for the previous seven years, always dreaming of the day I could move back to the country.

For our first date, Stuart stopped by my house on the morning after the office Christmas party. We had sat together on the bus that took the whole company to a dinner. As I was sitting at the kitchen table in my Boston house, drinking coffee and eating a bagel with him, I decided to fall in love with the man with red hair who lived in the only place I'd ever felt happy. He was charming enough then to make it easy to imagine. It wasn't love at first sight. That had already happened to me once, and I remember the great sweep of confusion, lust, and embarrassment because it had all seemed so crazy. No, this wasn't that. This was more calculated. This was red hair and a sparkly smile that could lead to a farm in the Adirondacks with a dog and a horse.

I sometimes wonder what I was for him. And at the risk of oversimplifying the answer, I would have to say it might just have been that his beloved wife, who had borne him his beloved son, had left him for another man. Her name was Susan, and we looked so much alike we could have been sisters. But maybe I'm wrong. Maybe I wasn't just the stand-in for the first Susan. But I know for sure that by the end of that breakfast, we both knew there was something between us.

We dated for a year; that is, once every two months or so, we'd spend a weekend together somewhere like Nantucket or skiing at Wildcat Mountain in New Hampshire and, finally, at his farm in the Adirondacks. It was a seven-hour drive from Boston, most of it up the Northway through some of the prettiest wilderness in America. I recognized the mountains I had climbed as a camper: Cascade, Marcy, Phelps, Algonquin. It was like coming home; I was in love with his place before I even saw it. It must have been spring, but I don't really remember. There are so many pines in the Adirondacks, the forests are green even in winter. There could have been snow on the ground, or there could have been lilacs blooming on the overgrown hedge between the road and his house. I was so thrilled to be back, I was lost in the memories and smells of camp.

What I do remember is the inside of the house. A two-hundred-year-old hand-hewn log cabin renovated by its owners, a husband and wife who were both architects. It was small, less than a thousand square feet, with an open floor plan downstairs, a large brick fireplace right in the middle of the room, and a loft area with two bedrooms upstairs. The inside walls were white stucco, and large windows opened onto rolling pastureland out to the high peaks in the distance. The electricity went out so often, the whole house was fitted with a backup system of gas lighting that gave it a warm yellow glow at night. Behind the house two maple trees grew through a large cedar deck, and past the deck was a small pond with a waterfall at one end, cascading into a narrow stream. Next to that was a weathered gray barn with an attached chicken coop, both in need of repair. The property was surrounded by Adirondack State Park on every side, and the nearest house was more than half a mile away. I loved it so much it hurt.

Stuart was renting the place with a handsome ski racer for a roommate, and from what I could tell, living there was one big party. Dirty dishes filled the sink and covered every inch of counter space. There was no food to speak of but plenty of wine, liquor, and beer. Clumps of dead flies lay in every windowsill, thick with dust. Don't even ask about the bathroom. But none of that bothered me, fastidious though I am. I saw only the potential. All weekend I imagined what I could do with the place if it were mine, starting with putting a horse or two in that sweet gray barn.

After that weekend, I dreamed of living on his farm and riding my horse on the old logging roads that disappeared for miles into the woods. I dreamed of raising chickens, swimming in the pond, and sitting in front of the fire in February with a howling wind outside and the soft hiss from the gaslights inside. I dreamed of quitting my job and sitting at a desk in the loft to write a book during the long, dark days of winter. I dreamed of marrying the man who rented that farm so he could give me happiness on top of all the happiness I would surely feel just living in such a place. Then something happened that put the dream within reach.

During our year of dating, we spoke on the phone far more often than we saw each other. He was always traveling, and my new job as a customer service manager for a ski company kept me busy, too, but after work, with a glass and a bottle of wine next to my phone and a bottle of Scotch next to his, we would talk late into the night. One such night, when we had been talking for hours, I suddenly had trouble breathing and had to put down the phone. I was a smoker and imagined I had finally done irreparable damage to my lungs. Frightened, I stood up and spent a minute or two bent over, unable to draw a single breath of air. When I could finally take a breath, I was so relieved I cried and right then made a promise to him that I would quit smoking.

Early the next morning, before I went to work, there was a knock at the front door. I opened it to find my aunt, who had come to tell me that my grandmother had died the night before. The time of her death was the exact moment I had suffered breathing trouble.

I was flooded with mixed feelings at the news. After the death of my mother and the disappearance of my father when I was five years old, this grandmother had become a legal guardian for my brother and me. She was rich, punitive, and domineering, and I had lived in terror of her for eighteen years until I had left for college and vowed never to see her again. But after that, I had seen her two or three times during brief visits urged on me by my brother or aunt, who insisted it was the right thing to do. I barely remember those visits, except that once she gave me some of her jewelry, which surprised me because I thought she hated me. I hardly knew what to say to her. Besides giving me Bunty when I was six, offering me jewelry had seemed like the nicest thing she had ever done.

I was even more confused when, a few weeks after her death, I discovered that she had left me a substantial inheritance. I could not recall hearing a single kind word from her, yet she had left me money. She had given me my independence. It was impossible to comprehend. I had lived in her grand houses and sat in the back of her chauffeured cars, but I had never thought I was part of that world because I never felt welcomed into her life. The only thing she communicated clearly to me was what a disappointment I was, how utterly I had failed her. This was repeated daily whenever I was in her presence or by mail if I was away at school or camp. I spent much of my life trying to undo the damage of that message. And yet, in leaving me money, she had given me a kind of freedom I could never have imagined and, certainly, could never have created on my own. I was filled with a stunned and guilty gratitude. Maybe she hadn't hated me after all. Would I ever be able to live up to her legacy?

I married the handsome red-haired stranger on the back deck of the log cabin, and a few days later I bought it. My grandmother would have reached out of her grave and grabbed the pen out of my hand if she had seen me put the beautiful Adirondack farm in both our names, mine and my husband's, as a loving and trusting gesture. My grandmother was a smart businesswoman and had known how to preserve her wealth over more than half a century. She wouldn't have put a doghouse in anyone else's name, let alone a hundred-acre farm. But I was determined not to go through life leaving a trail of hurt people behind the way my grandmother had, so I would be magnanimous. I would be kind.

Were we happy for a week? A month? Two months? Yes, it was about two months. The ski racer moved out, and I cleaned up the cabin. We ate wonderful dinners under the gaslights and drank every night until we passed out to-gether, and in the morning we told each other we had the flu, a cold, the runs, anything but a whopping hangover, and so it went, day after day after day. I bought a New-foundland puppy and named him Bear and one day brought two gray kittens home from the dump and named them Samantha and Zucchini. We hired a young man, Alan, to help us fix up the barn and chicken coop, and when it was finished, I went out and bought half a dozen chickens and one rooster. A few weeks later, a young woman asked if she could leave Nikka, her quarter-horse mare, in our barn while she was away at college, and a few weeks after that, I took in an old gelded Welsh pony named Thunder to keep Nikka company.

For a year I wrote letters to my brother and cousins in Boston telling them how happy I was. I sent them pictures of the horses and chickens and the little vegetable garden I had planted next to the waterfall and the cats sleeping on the open skylights in the roof, and the views of the mountains from our kitchen window and Bear looking big and goofy stretched across the stone stoop in front of the house. But it was all a lie, a terrible lie, because I left out the yelling and screaming and drunken beatings that had started in the first month of our marriage and had only gotten worse. I left out that I had married a monster.

Sitting in the sunroom with Holly after riding that day, I wondered if I had the courage to kill myself. With pills? By jumping from a high bridge? I sipped my tea, giggling quietly with Holly. My husband's hunting rifle?

My Newfoundland lay snoring on the cool tile floor next to my rocking chair when suddenly he looked up. I heard it too, a high-pitched buzz coming from somewhere over the treetops beyond the pasture. All three of us stared through the glass roof of the sunroom, and a few seconds later a small yellow biplane appeared like a smudge of bright crayon. We watched it inch high across the sky toward us until it was directly over the pasture, when it dipped its nose straight down and dived to the earth like a dropped garden trowel.

Holly and I screamed, partly in shock, partly in delight, because we knew who it was. We knew who had come to give us this private air show. No, it was not for me, not for *us*. This dance in the sky was for Holly. The yellow toy dived and spun and twirled, the horses in the pasture barely glancing up even as it buzzed so close we could see the white stripe that ran through the black strap on Mike's goggles. It was an open cockpit, and we could see the way the wind whipped at Mike's hair, how it billowed and snapped at his shirtsleeves. We could see him smile at Holly as he flew low over the pasture toward the sunroom, pulling into a steep climb just before killing himself and us, too — or so it seemed.

Who could have imagined such a thing? It was strange and thrilling. For a few minutes I forgot that I drank too much, that I hated the man who lay upstairs recovering from a heart attack at the age of thirty-six. I forgot about the nights I slept in the barn to avoid being hit. I forgot about the shame I felt at having chosen such a partner, at the enormity of my mistake; the job, the friends, the home I had left in Boston only the year before, the money I had spent to buy this farm and then to renovate it, all the while knowing I would have to leave, waiting for the courage to figure out where to go, what to do, how to live.

I had a horse now, an equine child to consider with her equine stepsiblings. In less than a week, Georgia had changed everything. It had taken almost a year to find her, but the connection to her felt old, as old as I was. She had awakened something inside me so intense, so profound, I wanted to do for her what I could not do for myself: I wanted to keep her safe. I wanted to change. It had already begun. *Alcoholic.* I had written it down, given it a dimension, an authority, something honest enough to terrify me.

But for a moment, watching the yellow airplane, I had forgotten about all of that. I had forgotten I wanted to die and was glad when the little plane didn't crash into the sunroom but, at the last minute, aimed its nose into the air and headed straight into what surely looked like oblivion.

{CHAPTER 2}

I HATED BEING AWAY from my animals, especially Georgia. She was the reason I could drag myself out of bed in the morning no matter how hung over I felt. She was why suddenly everything mattered again and why the status quo had become unbearable: my drinking, the yelling, the beatings. She had awakened something old and precious, feelings of wonder and hope and excitement. For years I had lived with the lethargy of alcoholism, its deadening blur the perfect solution for someone who couldn't quite push herself to be all dead, not forever and ever, as I imagined endlessly. I'd buried myself alive instead, peering out from behind the thick barrier of liquor, so nothing, no matter how ugly, was ever quite ugly enough.

Until Georgia. Falling in love with Georgia had jerked me awake, and once awake, I couldn't deny what I saw anymore. I couldn't deny the ugliness that was my life and the lies I had to tell to sustain it. The spring after Georgia arrived, I had to go on a business trip with my husband. It was the annual ski convention held in Las Vegas, and besides attending an endless round of cocktail parties, we were there to look at the latest lines of ski equipment and clothing we would sell to ski shops all over the East Coast. By then I'd been in the ski business for a couple of years and knew enough to realize it was the perfect career for an alcoholic. The industry is full of people who never want to grow up, who never want to leave the slightly glamorous life lived on the slopes of Vail or Aspen or White Face; they figure out that the best way to feel eighteen forever is to go from skiing all day and drinking all night to talking about skiing all day and still drinking all night. To be fair, there are some ordinary businessmen and -women making a living like any other adult. I was not one of them, and neither was my husband. We were good skiers, we liked to drink, and never growing up was fine with both of us. The ski show in Las Vegas was the ultimate pilgrimage for the most devoted. We fitted right in.

If Georgia's arrival had begun my awakening, Las Vegas was where any chance of my sleepwalking through life ended. It happened, not surprisingly, one night when I was drunk. During the day, my husband and I were good at maintaining a façade of congeniality. By then I knew I hated him and it was only a matter of time until I figured out how to end the marriage, but that didn't keep me from walking around the convention center with him, attending fashion shows and equipment demonstrations, holding his hand and smiling. Back at the hotel room after a night of partying with friends, it was different. Free from my obsessive need to keep up an appearance of normality, alone with him, I couldn't fake anything. So in a hotel room two thousand miles from home, with both of us falling down drunk, I introduced the idea of separating. And then his hands were around my neck.

I know I fought back because later the police told me that I'd bitten him all the way to the artery just above his wrist, the only place I could reach as I struggled to free myself from his stranglehold. I know I was more enraged than scared because when I screamed, according to the people in the next room who heard me and had called the police, I had screamed *No!* and not *Help!* over and over, and I was still screaming it when the police kicked in the door and pulled Stuart away from me.

My husband was taken to the hospital, and after I stubbornly refused to press charges, I was driven to another hotel to spend the rest of the night with one of my best friends and her husband. The next day I flew back to Massachusetts with this couple and stayed with them until I could figure out what to do next. Sally was one of the first people to know the truth about my marriage, although I never told her about my own drinking. I don't know whether she knew anyway, but she never mentioned it, only encouraging me to leave Stuart before it was too late.

During the first few days in the calm, safe environment of Sally's house, I didn't drink as much, and with the relative clarity that came from being less drunk, I realized that, plan or no plan about where to go next, my marriage was over and I would never spend another night with Stuart in the farmhouse in the Adirondacks. Then a kind of peace came over me. No matter how anxious I felt about the future, the thought that it wouldn't include this man was liberating.

After a few days at Sally's, the phone calls started. With forty-five stitches in his wrist and a brand-new conscience, Stuart called to say he was sorry and that it would never happen again.

What won't happen? I asked. In the past he hadn't remembered being physically violent, and I wondered if this time was any different, if he remembered that he had tried to kill me.

Hitting, he said.

So he didn't remember. He hadn't hit me in Las Vegas; he had wrapped his hands around my neck and squeezed.

I know you miss Georgia, he said, ramping up the conciliatory tone in his voice. *At least come back to see her and then we can talk. I'll understand whatever you decide to do. I promise.*

It sounded so reasonable. I'd go back and tell him we'd made a terrible mistake in marrying. We'd agree on who owned what, and after the talk was over, we'd shake hands, and one of us would leave to stay with friends until whoever that person was could find someplace else to live.

Okay, I said. *Just talk.*

Just talk, he assured me.

Sally drove me to the airport in Albany to pick up the car where we'd left it the week before, which seemed like a lifetime ago. On the way there, she tried to talk me out of going back. *Don't go,* she said. *Hitters don't change, especially not overnight.*

But Sally hadn't heard how reasonable his voice had sounded, and she didn't know how much I missed Georgia. *I'll be okay,* I insisted. In the back of my mind I realized I didn't want Stuart to be alone with my animals. I knew that he might be a danger to them, but I couldn't see that he was a danger to me as well.

An hour before I arrived home, I pulled to the side of the road and wrote my husband a letter. I was afraid that in the heat of the moment I wouldn't be able to express my feelings, and I wanted to tell him clearly and without anger the reasons why I was leaving. In the letter I acknowledged for the first time that I had a drinking problem, too, and that because of it our fights had grown out of control and dangerous. I told him that the reason I hadn't pressed charges in Las Vegas or any of the other times that he had been violent was that I didn't want to do anything that would hurt his business or his standing in the community. And although there was some truth in that, the real reason was that I was too ashamed to tell anyone my husband was hitting me.

The letter was short, and I finished it by telling him that I was sorry the dream we shared about living on our beautiful farm together in the Adirondacks had ended so quickly and disastrously. I told him I was sorry if I had ever hurt him. I folded the letter into my pocket and pulled out on the road to drive the rest of the way home.

I turned into the driveway in the early evening, and leaving the luggage in the car to unpack later, I walked into the house to find my husband. He was in the kitchen cooking dinner, and when he saw me, he walked across the living room with his bandaged wrist visible under his shirt cuff and hugged me hello. His touch sickened me, but I tried not to show it, resting my hands on his arms until he pulled away.

I made your favorite meal, he said, turning around and walking back to the kitchen to show me. The stovetop was covered with simmering pots, and the whole house smelled of garlic and butter. I stood on the dining room side of the stove, nodding and smiling to let him know I appreciated the effort.

I wrote you something, I said, handing him the letter across a frying pan of chicken breasts smothered in butter, white wine, and shallots. *Smells good,* I added, closing my eyes and breathing in the savory smells.

You bitch, he snarled, crumpling up the letter after he had read it and throwing it across the stove into my startled face.

It took a second to register that my letter had the opposite effect of what I had intended. It took less than that to see his hand move toward the knife rack; I turned and ran back across the living room toward the garage. As I ran, I could feel my body shaking in terror, but even so, once in the garage, I managed to control my shaking hand long enough to lock the door behind me before I threw myself into the car and left a cloud of burning rubber as I exploded the car backward and shot out of the garage.

As far as I know, my husband never made it out of the house. I didn't see him in the rearview mirror, but I didn't slow down to make sure. I drove ninety miles an hour on the narrow country road that led away from our house until the first turn, where I slowed down just enough not to slam myself into the tall pines crowding the side of the road that led straight to Lake Placid. As soon as I was safely through the turn, I was back up to ninety, my pulse reverberating in my ears as if I were swimming under water. I didn't know where I was going, but I knew I couldn't slow down until there were people and buildings around. I couldn't slow down until I found help.

It was ten miles to Lake Placid, and by the time I arrived on the outskirts, I was calm enough to begin thinking straight. I couldn't go to the police because I had no proof that he had chased me out of the house with a knife. I had no proof that he had ever threatened me or hit me because I had never been willing to file charges. Even in Las Vegas, at my own insistence, the incident had been recorded only as a domestic disturbance. It was 1980, years before the police were trained to handle domestic violence as anything other than a waste of their time or a nuisance unless you were standing in front of them bleeding and bruised. No, I drove right past the police station knowing I couldn't face the skeptical eyes and the indifferent shrugs as I tried to explain that I was chased out of my house at knifepoint.

I calmed down enough to drive through town sanely, sticking to the speed limit and stopping at traffic lights. But where was I going? Somehow, in my fantasy of what postmarriage life would look like, I had imagined keeping the house. I would also keep the horses, the dog, and the cats. It would be me not just because I had paid for it all but because I loved it more. He didn't care nearly as much about the farm as I did, and he certainly didn't care about the animals. But I realized there was little chance he would ever let me come back. He was too angry and too proud.

Suddenly I knew where to go. I knew that the only person who would understand exactly what I had gone through was my husband's ex-wife, Susan. Not only would she understand, but my husband would never think to look there, so I would be safe. She lived in Saranac Lake with her new husband, about fifteen miles from Lake Placid. During the past year, we had developed a friendship over the phone as we coordinated weekends to share custody of my six-year-old stepson. Susan and her husband owned a health food store and often brought bags of groceries for us when they dropped Eric off. I returned their generosity by giving them ski equipment and clothing, and we had established a distant but real friendship.

I drove to their house now, a large Victorian with a wraparound porch on the side of a hill in the middle of town. It was dinnertime when I knocked on the door, and Susan appeared wearing an apron and carrying a wooden spoon. One look at my face and she knew.

He hit you, she said, pulling me inside, closing and locking the door behind us.

How did you know? I asked, fighting back tears of shame and relief.

Don't worry, she said. *John will kill him if he tries to come here.* John was Susan's husband, a tall and muscular man but so gentle he wouldn't kill an ant. I knew she meant I was safe with them. I could stay.

I don't remember how long I stayed. A few days? A week? I remember only that they were kind and I told them everything. Almost everything. I never mentioned that I was an alcoholic. I couldn't imagine telling anyone. While there, I drank less, careful never to get sloppy.

Susan and I spent a lot of time together talking. She told me how she and my husband had met while working at a small ski area in Vermont. They'd fallen in love quickly and married a year later in a beautiful ceremony on the ski slope. The hitting started as soon as they were married, but by then she was already pregnant and didn't dare leave. Things got better when their son was born, and for a while the hitting stopped. She showed me her photo album from that time, and their lives looked happy and full of friendships and good times. I would never have guessed from looking at her photos that underneath it all, a nightmare was festering.

It wasn't just the hitting, it was the rage, she said. *I knew someday I'd leave, but I had a baby, no money, and no place to go.*

John was a friend she knew from church, and when the hitting started again, she went to the minister and to John for help. What followed was a year of stalking, terrifying threats, calls to the police, and an upheaval of their whole community as they tried to deal with the out-of-control behavior of a man who, a few years later, would do the same thing to me.

As I listened to Susan's story, I knew that my divorce would be hers, that Stuart's anger would stand in the way of negotiating a reasonable settlement without a lawyer and maybe even without the police. In hindsight, the hope that I could hand him a note and we'd be able to sit down and discuss the rest seemed absurd. In talking to Susan I realized that I could never be alone with my husband again. I could never even let him know where I lived.

Friends who had just bought a house in Lake Placid still owned another house in Connecticut that they were trying to sell. They offered me the Connecticut house as a place to stay until it sold. I accepted their offer with a mix of gratitude and enormous sadness. I had no idea what the future held, but I knew that if I moved to Connecticut,

I wasn't going to be reunited with Georgia soon and I'd probably never live in Lake Placid again. I knew I had lost the farm.

When I had fled the house at knifepoint, I'd fled in a car full of luggage from my trip to Las Vegas. So although most of my clothes, the animals, and all of my other possessions were still at the house in Lake Placid, I had enough to manage until I could figure out a way to collect the rest. Alone at the house in Connecticut, I agonized about the animals. Was he taking care of them? Would he hurt Georgia as a way to get back at me? Even if I could take them, where would I put them? My friends didn't want dogs or cats in the house while they were trying to sell it. And their manicured front lawn was no place for horses. It was a formal house with white pillars in front, lots of white wall-to-wall carpeting, and a swimming pool surrounded by an elaborate flower garden. It was completely empty, so I bought a mattress and put it on the floor of the master bedroom. That was where I ate, slept, drank, and every night cried myself to sleep missing Georgia.

I thought I had plenty of money, until a few days after moving to Connecticut, as I was filling up the car with gas, I discovered my credit card had been canceled. All of my credit cards had been canceled. They were joint credit cards, just like my checking and savings accounts, just like the car loan, which was in both of our names, just like the house and the business and everything I owned. I had nothing that belonged just to me, and suddenly I had nothing at all. While I had been worrying about the animals and wondering where I'd go when the house in Connecticut sold, he'd gone to the bank.

I needed a lawyer, but I didn't have enough money to

hire one. I didn't even have enough money to buy a tuna fish sandwich. I didn't know what to do or whom to ask for help. I'd hardly told a soul about what had happened or where I was living. I had run away and hidden because I didn't know what else to do. I didn't trust the law to protect me from a man like my husband, and certainly no one in my family or any of my friends could. Back then, there were no options for a woman trying to get away from a battering spouse except to leave and try to begin her life over again where he couldn't find her.

A good friend named Tim, whom I knew from the ski business, helped me find a lawyer, who did what lawyers do: he went to court and secured enough money to pay himself a retainer and for me to live on for a while. That was the beginning of what would be a contentious, year-long divorce process that Stuart's rage made as difficult as possible every step of the way.

A few months after I moved to Connecticut, the house sold and I had to find another place to live. During those months there, Tim and I had started to date. He was going through a divorce, too, though it was far less contentious than mine. So Tim suggested looking for a house in the Catskills — we both loved to ski, and it was an easy drive from where he lived in New Jersey. I rented a place in Woodstock, and just after moving there, I found out my husband was going into a Boston hospital for heart surgery. While he was in the hospital, I rented a U-Haul truck, and with Tim and four of his biggest male friends, drove to the farm in Lake Placid and retrieved my dog, the cats, the furniture, and everything else I owned before I had married him. I still hadn't found a place to keep a horse, and it broke my heart not to be able to bring Georgia that night. It took us all night to pack the truck, and I became so drunk I don't remember most of it. We had expected to find people living at the house, possibly friends of my husband's he would have "hired" to live there while he was in the hospital in the event I planned to do exactly what I did. But there was no one at the house to stop us, and by seven the next morning, as the truck pulled out of the driveway and headed south, I was passed out between my dog and Tim's shoulder.

When we had first arrived with the truck, I'd gone to see Georgia right away. There were no lights in the barn, and she spooked when she saw me, almost running me down as she fled into the pasture. I walked out and stood nearby, waiting for her to calm down and approach me when she was ready. I hadn't seen her in several months, and I was worried she wouldn't remember me. I stood still, calling her name and shaking a bag of carrots to entice her to come. She danced around me in big circles, snorting her alarm at the dark figure standing in the middle of her pasture. Obviously she wasn't used to night visitors, but I was desperate to see her. I was desperate to see if she looked well taken care of, if her weight was normal, and if there were any signs that someone was grooming her and keeping her feet trimmed.

Finally she approached me, the sound of carrots in a plastic bag impossible for her to resist. I said her name softly, stroking her neck and giving her a carrot as soon as she came near. I could hardly see, so I ran my hand down her neck to the top of her shoulder and then all the way down her back and underneath to her belly. She felt OK. Silky and smooth and not too ribby. She turned her head to watch me, chewing her carrot but no longer alarmed about who I was or what I was doing in her pasture in the middle of the night. Still, I had no idea if she remembered me, but she must have felt I was a benevolent presence. She must have felt, at least a little, the enormous wave of love being sent her way. We'd been together only five months before I'd left, but it felt as though we'd been together my whole life.

I cried on her neck, smelling her familiar musk and feeling I had let her down in every possible way. If I could have gotten her bridle and saddle and ridden her away that night to a safe place, I would have. But I had nowhere to take her and no way to take care of her. I could only wait and trust my lawyer, who assured me bringing her back would be easy. In the meantime, I told her, I would buy a place for us. I would buy another farm and never, not for the rest of her life, leave her again.

Within a few minutes, Nikka and Thunder came out of the barn and joined us in the middle of the pasture. They jostled together, pushing their noses at the bag of carrots, insisting on sharing the treat. I had plenty, and while I was handing them out, I slipped my leg over the back of Thunder and sat on him while they finished eating. He didn't mind and shuffled away to graze while the other two followed. It was a moonless night, but even in the dark I could see the shape of the barn at the edge of the pasture and the outline of the house farther up the hill and beyond it. I could hear the waterfall at the end of the pond as it splashed over the dam to the stream below and the trill of crickets like a thousand whistling teapots floating across the warm night air.

I knew I was leaving the Adirondacks for good. What had happened in this place had changed everything. The dream I had cherished and then built was broken. It wasn't just that a dangerous man lived there; it was also because of what I'd done and who I had become. I was the monster I was trying to escape from, and the farm in Lake Placid had become a reminder of that monster. How could I have abandoned my dog and my horse and everything that was dearest to me? How could I have ruined the life I'd been desperate to live since I was a child? How could I have lost my grandmother's money? I was so filled with shame and self-hatred I could hardly breathe. So instead I drank. And drank and drank and drank.

I came to slumped against the truck door at the Americana Hotel outside Albany, where the moving men had stopped to wash up and eat breakfast. They asked if I wanted anything, and I said no and passed out again until three hours later, when we pulled into the driveway of the rental house in Woodstock. They unloaded everything into the enormous three-car garage, and when they left, I went into the house and sank into the worst depression I'd ever known. Having Bear and my cats was only a small comfort, and Georgia was still in Lake Placid. I didn't know what my husband would do in retaliation after he discovered that I'd taken my things out of the house, but I knew it wouldn't be good, and I was afraid it might involve Georgia.

I drank myself into a stupor that night, but no amount of alcohol could quell the fear of what lay ahead. During the day, fighting terrible hangovers, I looked at houses with real estate agents. At night I tried to drink away my depression and fears about my horse and everything else. I had no job, no friends, and no idea how to pick up the pieces and begin my life over again. I knew I had a drinking problem, but I still hadn't connected it to all the other problems in my life. I saw them as separate issues — there was the drinking issue, and then there were all the other problems. Alcoholism is an amazing obfuscator.

One night, while drinking alone in my house, I felt I couldn't stand being separated from Georgia another day. I called a friend in Lake Placid whose teenage daughter had often come to ride with me in the past. June was a vivacious, friendly girl whom my husband and I had both liked a lot. I told the mother I was divorcing and had moved but that my husband still had Georgia. I didn't tell her I had left because he was violent, and I didn't tell her I had "stolen" all my things in the middle of the night. I asked her if she'd be willing to let June go to the house and ask to take Georgia on a trail ride so I could then meet her at predetermined place with a horse trailer. No matter what happened, I was sure my husband would never do anything to hurt June. His violent outbursts seemed to be reserved for his wives, the only two people he had ever hit. The mother understood messy divorces and was sympathetic to my situation; she agreed to let her daughter do this for me.

I hired a horse trailer, but at the last minute listened to my lawyer's advice and decided not to make the trip myself. My lawyer said it was unsafe for me to go anywhere near my husband. I told the driver what was happening and where to meet June. Tim couldn't go either, but one of the guys who had helped us move volunteered to keep the driver company and to help load Georgia. I located a stable close to the rental house where I could keep a horse until I found a place of my own. It all seemed perfect.

I was a nervous wreck. I stayed close to the phone in case the two men got lost or couldn't load Georgia. But the crisis that happened was not the one I had anticipated. The phone call came at about three in the afternoon; it was June's mother, and she was angry. Her daughter had gone to my house and asked my husband if she could take Georgia out for a ride. He'd said yes, and she'd gone to the barn to brush Georgia and tack her up. June was so eager to please me, she decided to steal as much of Georgia's paraphernalia as she could. She left Georgia's halter on under the bridle and then loaded herself up with brushes, lead lines, hoof picks, fly spray, a fly hood, and even a bright red ball of vet wrap. By the time she left the barn, there was stuff hanging all over Georgia's saddle, and June's pockets were bulging. My husband had seen her leave the barn from the house and knew immediately what she was doing.

He waited until she had crossed the road and disappeared into the woods, then jumped in the car and drove to where he assumed the trailer would be waiting. He had guessed right. There it was. He tried to beat up the driver (so much for believing he attacked only his wives), but between the driver and Tim's friend, they were able to hold him off. He refused to leave until June appeared with Georgia a short while later, at which point he threatened her, too, but the other two men intervened and June was left untouched. He made her dismount from the horse and waited until they had all driven away in the trailer before he rode Georgia back to the farm himself. The whole operation had been an unmitigated disaster, and on top of it, I had been wrong to assume my husband wouldn't try to hurt June. I had put my dear friend in harm's way.

It wasn't just that I had put my friend's daughter in danger, it was also the image of my husband grabbing Georgia's bridle and throwing himself into the saddle to ride her back to the farm that kept me awake that night. In his anger, I was sure he had hurt her. I was sure he had yelled and jerked her mouth and kicked her hard, and God knows what else, because to him Georgia was just an extension of me and as good a thing to pound as any. It made me sick to think about it, and several times during the night I had to pace and breathe through the idea that I'd left my horse with such a man.

Tim tried to help me through the depression, but he was going through his own divorce and had enough problems to handle. He'd already done a lot to help me move and send a friend to help with Georgia; I didn't want to obligate myself to him any more than I already had. So mostly I was on my own. I was a wreck and in no shape to get a job. At night I drank until I passed out and then spent the next morning trying to recover. I would have been completely alone if I hadn't spent most afternoons with a realtor looking at houses. I didn't know anyone in the Woodstock area, and since I was hiding from my husband, I hadn't given my address to any friends; I used a post office box in the next town as a mailing address.

To throw my husband further off the trail, at my lawyer's suggestion, I rented an apartment in the Albany area that would serve the additional purpose of requiring that my husband come to court in Albany. The apartment was in a three-story walkup in a down-at-the-heels neighborhood, and I stayed in it only long enough to install a phone and an answering machine before leaving and never going back. It seemed a terrible waste of money, but I did what my lawyer told me. I was afraid that if I didn't, I'd never see Georgia again.

At night I lay in bed in the rental house listening to mice scurry through the walls, wondering if the good part of my life was over and from then on it was going to be more of this hell. I wasn't numb from the liquor, I was numb from spending my life looking for something I could barely articulate but in my mind had reduced to calling home. I was numb from living so much of my life in fear, beginning with the grandmother who had become my guardian and, most recently, a violent man.

I wanted to find my home — the place where, for the first time, I would feel a sense of peace and safety and belonging, a place free from fear. I knew such feelings existed because I had felt them at the camp I attended for nine straight summers, a camp nestled at the foot of Trouble and Balance Rock Mountains in the heart of the Adirondacks. I'd known the love of a horse there, too, and in finding Georgia, I had exceeded my wildest dreams in bringing back the joy, pleasure, and comfort that living with a horse could bring. I knew that whatever happened next in my life, it would have to include Georgia. Maybe she was the wrong thing to be fighting for. Maybe I should have been fighting for the house and the money and part of the ski business. But she's what mattered most because in loving Georgia, for the first time I felt I had the foundation on which to build my home.

{ CHAPTER 3 }

ON A SNOWY DAY in December, nine months after leaving Lake Placid, I was lost in the Catskills trying to find the house I'd just bought in a town called Olivebridge, seventeen miles from Woodstock. Ahead of me wound a dark narrow road through a forest of snow-covered pines, and behind me followed a moving van filled with everything I owned. We'd driven around icy back roads between Woodstock and Olivebridge for three hours looking for the new house because I couldn't remember the name of the road it was on. All the documents that might have told me were packed in a box somewhere in the back of the moving van among dozens of other boxes.

A call to the realtor, in those days, meant first finding a phone booth at a little general store in the middle of no-where, leaving a message on her answering machine, and then waiting nearby in the car hoping she would call back. It was December 23, and I didn't know that the realtor was long gone, already celebrating Christmas with her family in Bermuda.

We waited in the deepening afternoon gloom, ner-vously watching snow accumulate on the roof of the phone booth that wouldn't ring. After an hour, the driver of the moving van swung himself down from the cab and, leaving deep footprints in the fresh snow as he crossed the road, leaned into my window and suggested I find a hotel for the night and resume the search the next day. He clearly had no idea whom he was talking to, or that the smiley, apologetic woman in the driver's seat of the old manure-smelling Subaru station wagon had been searching for home not for three hours, as he reasonably assumed, but ever since the sudden loss of her first home twenty-eight years earlier.

In the middle of the night the phone rings. I am wearing one-piece pajamas with feet, and my brother is wearing something with cowboys on it. We have been running around giggling all night, thrilled and confused that we are getting away with being out of bed. The wall phone in the kitchen is too high for either one of us to reach, so when it rings, Lloyd drags a stool across the floor and tries to climb up. But the stool has no low rungs to put his foot on, so by the time he makes it to the seat and picks up the phone, the person on the other end has hung up. This hap-pens two or three more times, with the same result.

Between rings, we tiptoe to the door of our father's room to see if he's awake. He is wearing boxer shorts and lies spread out on the bare mattress, snoring loudly. There is a red, heart-shaped box of chocolates lying open on his bureau — a Valentine's gift, but from whom? Our mother has been dead for a week.

She died, he had told us, sitting between us on the couch in the playroom, staring at his shoes. I had stared at his shoes, too, wondering if they had something to do with what he was saying. *Died,* he had said again and stood up and left.

Every time we come to the doorway of our sleeping father, we reach inside and take a piece of chocolate out of the box. There are hardly any left, and I worry about what will happen when he wakes up and finds them gone. I know we will lie and say we've never seen them.

My father's room smells of cigarettes and something sweet. Not the chocolates, something else. I think it has to do with the bottle of gold liquid on the floor next to the bed. No matter how much noise we make, he doesn't wake up. At some point we must have fallen asleep because the next time we look in his bedroom, our father is gone.

Hours or days go by, and we are still alone in the house. We stay in our pajamas and eat cereal and watch television. We make peanut-butter-and-jelly sandwiches, which we have never done before. There are dirty plates and glasses, and sugar and cereal are spilled all over the counter. I feed the dog Milk-Bone biscuits and bologna. We let her into the backyard to pee, and when she comes inside, she lies on the floor with us in front of the television. It doesn't occur to us to call anyone; besides, we don't know how. We don't get dressed and we don't go outside. Neither of us knows how to tell time, but it doesn't matter because time has stopped. We leave the television only to get something to eat or to use the bathroom.

It is night again, and the wind is blowing so hard we can see the willow tree in the backyard bend to the ground. The rain pours down the window panes. Suddenly the lights go out, and it is completely dark. It is scary without the sound of the television filling the house. We stand at the window and can just make out a big branch from the willow break off with a cracking sound.

We hear a car door slam and run to the windows at the front of the house. We can see by the headlights that it is Grandmother Richards's car, and we watch her chauffeur, Franz, get out, holding a big wicker basket. He comes through the kitchen door, stamps his feet on the doormat, and wipes the rain from his clothes. He takes off his chauffeur's cap and shakes it out in the sink.

Mon, vhat a mess, he says when he sees the sink. He has a German accent. He pulls a big flashlight out of the basket and tells us to stay in the kitchen with the dog. We sit at a red child-size table and watch the beam of light bounce across the checked dining room floor and then down the hall toward our bedrooms. When he comes back, the wicker basket is full of our clothes. He puts his cap on and carries the basket to the car. Then he comes back and tells us he will carry us one at a time. The power lines are down, and if we step on them, Franz says, we will die.

There's that word again.

He lifts me up in my dirty pajamas and carries me into the rain and wind. In the back seat of the car is a blanket, and he tells me to pull it across my lap. A few minutes later Lloyd is next to me, and then Franz is sliding into the front seat and slamming shut his door.

What about Lulie? I ask.

No dog, he says and starts backing out of the driveway.

My eyes are frozen on the silver ashtray protruding from the seat in front of me. Who will sleep with me? Who will give Lulie her Milk-Bones?

The tires make a hissing sound against the wet roads, and I can smell my grandmother's flowery perfume on the blanket. Sometimes I glimpse a branch in the window above me, but the only way I know for sure we are moving is when the car rounds a corner and I fall against my brother, who shoves me away, a little harder each time.

Twenty minutes later Franz pulls into the garage, and I can see my grandmother's blue hair as she stands in the doorway leading to the laundry room. She is not German but says something to Franz in German and then switches to English to tell my brother and me to go straight to our rooms for bed. We have never been upstairs in her house and don't know where our rooms are. She doesn't hug us or smile or ask if we're hungry. I am, but I don't tell her. We follow her into the kitchen. Franz is behind us with the basket and tells her he will take us upstairs. They are speaking German again, and Franz keeps looking at us and shaking his head. They don't want us here.

I smell my grandmother's perfume as we follow Franz up a wide curving staircase, past a long tapestry of deer running through the woods and then past a nook full of her treasures. This is as far as we have ever gone in her house, just up the stairs enough to look at the little statues and crooked bowls that she says are very, very old and can't be touched. Franz says it now. *Don't touch.* But if he wasn't here, we would.

My bedroom is first, bigger than the one at home, with twin beds side by side and a little bureau in between. *With a reading light,* Franz says. I don't know how to read and wonder if I'm allowed to turn it on anyway. He takes my half of the clothes out of the basket and puts them on the bed in a pile. Then he points to a bureau and says, *Put them away. Neatly.*

Lloyd follows him out of the room, and Franz shuts the door behind them. I go to the window, but it is too dark to see anything. I open every bureau drawer to see if there's anything inside. They're all empty, so I take things from the pile on the bed and put a few in each drawer. I wonder if I am doing it right.

Next to the closet is an open door that leads to a bathroom. I walk in and turn on the water in the bathtub. A centipede falls out of the tap, followed by dark brown water. I turn the water off quickly and run out of the bathroom with my heart pounding. What if the centipede climbs out of the tub? I scramble onto the bed and get under the covers, leaving the lights on as I've been doing ever since my mother stopped coming home. I don't have Lulie, and I don't have my stuffed bear, Toboe, yet either. I am about to cry when I notice a button on the wall right next to my bed. I reach out and push it, expecting the reading light to go on or maybe a light somewhere else, but nothing happens, so I push it again and then a few more times, and then I give up and snuggle deep into the bed, clutching a corner of the blanket.

A few minutes later the door explodes open and a red-faced Franz stalks into the room holding a screwdriver and a hammer. He reaches under the covers and yanks me out of bed by my arm. I scream, thinking he's going to hit me with the hammer, but he drags me to the middle of the room and bends down to yell close to my face, *You think you're a prima donna? You can just order Franz around?*

I pee in my pajamas, feeling the hot urine running down my legs, pooling into the feet. Franz doesn't notice and leaves me sobbing in the middle of the room; he goes to the wall next to my bed, to the little button, and shoves the screwdriver into the wall next to it, pounding it in with the hammer. Little sparks fly out of the wall and then smoke. My grandmother is standing in the doorway, yelling in German. He yells back and starts pulling wires and finally the button itself, right out of the wall. Where it used to be is a gaping, jagged hole. With the wires and button still dangling in his hand, Franz marches by me and then pushes past my grandmother in the doorway, both of them still yelling. Just before they disappear down the hall, he reaches back and slams the door shut.

I stand in the middle of the room with my chest heaving, tears and snot running into my mouth and down the front of my pajamas. I don't dare move. I don't even dare lower my chin to see where I have wet on the rug. My pajamas stick to my legs, cold now where the urine has soaked them, cold all around my feet. I stand there a long time, long enough to stop crying, long enough to believe no one is coming back, not my grandmother, not Franz, not Lloyd, not my father, not my mother. Not anyone. No one will take care of me. I understand that for the first time. Not here, not anywhere, not ever.

When I start to shiver, I walk to the bed and get under

the covers still wearing the cold wet pajamas. I fall asleep sucking on the satin edge of the wool blanket next to my cheek.

When Franz sees me in the kitchen the next morning, he points to me and says to the cook, *She thinks she's a prima donna.* The cook shakes her head and laughs. I don't know what a prima donna is, but I know it's not good. In front of the cook on the wall above the counter, near where she is setting a tray with silverware, there is a glass box full of numbers on the end of metal posts. Suddenly the box rings and one of the numbers pops up. It is number three. The cook points to the box and says to me, *That's your grandmother's bedroom. She wants her breakfast tray.*

Suddenly I understand about the button in my room. I understand that it is connected to this glass box in the kitchen. I understand why. I understand everything. I even understand what a prima donna is. And I understand that nobody in this kitchen knows me. And if I explain, which I don't, they still won't know me. Nobody will take care of me. Not here, not anywhere, not ever, because this is not my home. I understand that I am someone who has no home.

The driver of the moving van had no idea that at that moment I had more in common with the lunatic fringe than with the woman leading a truck with no snow tires and three tired men on a merry chase through a snow-storm. Anyway, finding a hotel would have been just as hard. We were lost.

I don't remember what I said to the driver's tired eyes as I watched the snowflakes cling to his hair and fall inside the collar of his coat. I must have lied. I must have said something like, *We're almost there* or *It's not far* or *I just remembered* . . . Whatever it was, the lunatic was in charge, and we would find my house or skid into a snowdrift trying.

Less than an hour later we did have an accident, but not the kind I had feared. We accidentally found the house. We took a left and turned a corner, and there it was, sitting in an open field, a small red converted barn with Bear's pond behind it and the big stone walls and the promise of a different future. I already felt it. Violence was something I had known in one form or another since I was five years old. That had ended. It was the biggest part of what made this house home; it was safe. It was all mine. It was a miracle.

Olivebridge had been an accident, too. I'd never heard of it. And even if I had, it wouldn't have occurred to me to live there. There was no town, no stores or restaurants, no sidewalks, only a few hundred people scattered on small farms or tucked into the woods in a corner of the Catskill Mountains that couldn't even claim tourist traffic.

I had moved there because of Tim. Not an important man, not one likely to become the next husband or the next big love, but the transition man, the one who stood by me as I went from married to divorced, from the Adirondacks to the Catskills, and eventually from drunk to sober. He was in transition, too, going through a divorce, searching for his own way forward, and for a while we stumbled along together. He had mentioned Woodstock as an interesting town, close enough to places we both liked: Hunter Mountain for skiing, New Jersey where he lived and worked, and New York City for everything under the sun. At his suggestion, I had rented the house in Woodstock while I looked for a house to buy.

At the time, I didn't have my horses and didn't know if I was ever going to have them again; nonetheless, I told the realtor I needed pasture fencing, a barn, and water. Oh, and some sort of modest house. A six-month search began in Woodstock and expanded outward in a twenty-mile radius, which eventually included Olivebridge. When she showed me my house, it was one of the few times in my life I trusted my gut on something. *Buy this house,* my gut had said, loud enough for me to hear it over the jabber of fears about spending the last of my money on something that so imperfectly met my needs; there was no barn or fencing around any of the twelve acres, and it was far from friends, family, or any place familiar.

Bear had been with me, and when we pulled into the driveway to look at the house for the first time, he had hopped out of the car and gone straight for a swim. I watched his roly-poly paddle across the small pond, listening to the phrase *buy this house* in my head, aware of a great stillness, all those stone walls, old, immovable, and silent, like Stonehenge, giants of endurance through the chaos of history, still there, still standing, ready to receive the next wave of pilgrims searching for who knew what. *Slow down,* they seemed to insist. What you do here will matter. Four days later I owned the house, the first bit of real peace I'd ever known.

There might have been peace all around me, but there was little of it inside me. For over a year I'd been promising myself I'd quit drinking, ever since writing the word *alcoholic* in my journal during the last months of my marriage. I'd never written the word again, but I knew what I knew. There was no going back. During those first days in Olivebridge, I marveled at the new house, at the peace and quiet and beauty of the fields divided by their stone walls. I marveled at the newly sanded wide-planked floors I ran across barefoot in the morning to grab the first aspirin of the day out of the medicine cabinet in the little bathroom off the master bedroom. I marveled at the spiral staircase that looked suspended in midair above the living room, a grown-up jungle gym for its wobbly occupant, who gripped the banister tightly each night. I marveled at my aloneness, safe from any kind of attack, including those about my drinking. I was free to drink myself to death if I wanted. I was free to break all my own promises: *I'll only drink wine; I'll only drink after 5 P.M.; I'll only drink one glass; I'll drink half a gallon of water before bed; I'll eat more leafy greens; I'll take milk thistle to protect my liver; I'll stop.*

In the morning, after gobbling aspirin, I'd feed the dog and drag myself to the road to run the obligatory four miles around "the block." Sometimes I'd throw up in the bushes along the way, and sometimes I'd have such strong heart palpitations, I'd wonder if I was just going to keel over and die face-down in the road. Every morning I pushed myself to finish the run, and every morning I swore I'd never drink again. By midday I'd be coherent enough to call my lawyer about the return of Georgia.

You have to give up on this, he'd say. *It's costing you a fortune, and your husband isn't going to relent. It would be cheaper to buy another horse.*

I'd grip the phone with sweaty hands and try not to let my lawyer know how unhinged I felt, how ashamed I was for marrying a man who would take a horse he didn't want, who would be so vindictive.

He can have whatever he wants, I'd say. *Just get the horse.*

But it's your money, he'd insist, and then more softly, *I know you love this horse, but you're going to need something to live on. You can't let him have it all.*

By then I'd be crying. I had already thrown away so much of my grandmother's money, and it looked as though I'd be throwing away what little was left because I couldn't live without my horse. I couldn't live without Georgia.

Please, I'd say and hang up before he tried to reason with me again.

I couldn't help it. I didn't want another horse. I wanted Georgia. I wanted the only horse who had made my heart jump at the first sight of her, who had made me want to find a safer, saner life. I needed the horse whom I loved enough to want to change myself, to stop lying to myself about my marriage, my drinking, and my pretend happiness on the farm in the Adirondacks. Having Georgia had done that for me in a way nothing else had. Finding her had been like getting Bunty twenty-five years earlier. Suddenly a door had opened, an escape hatch from the prison of a bad marriage. I could move again. I could get up, go to the barn, and get on my horse and go. I could surround myself with her smell and be comforted. I could feel my humanness in the presence of her horsiness. I was not a monster. I was someone who could love deeply. I was someone who loved Georgia.

The trouble was I didn't have Georgia. I had found the house, but without Georgia it wasn't quite a home yet. I loved my dog, who loved his pond and loved to amble with me through the woods and fields surrounding the property. But we were a lonely pair, incomplete without our bossy equine muse. When I looked out the living-room window across the pond and into the lush back fields, I could see her clearly in my mind's eye. I could see her gallop across the field to the pasture gate, not yet built, to greet me standing there with carrots, saddle, and bridle, ready for the morning ride we both loved. There was a beautiful view across the property, but every time I looked, it tugged at my heart because I mostly saw what wasn't there. It was hard to believe it had been nine months since our last ride. My lawyer promised he would get her back, but only if I didn't interfere with any more harebrained schemes of my own.

Be patient, he said. *Let me negotiate a settlement.*

Georgia's absence wasn't the only thing that kept the new house from feeling the way I imagined a home would feel. I knew if I didn't stop drinking, no place I lived in could soothe the craziness I felt inside. But I didn't know how to stop. It seemed impossible to decide not to drink one night and simply put down the bottle. I'd tried it a hundred times and never once succeeded.

Then in mid-April, a drinking friend from Boston came to visit and after a weekend spent doing what we did best, leaned across the kitchen counter Monday morning, pale and shaky, and made me promise I'd stop drinking with her. I was shocked at the idea but agreed just to be polite. I had no intention of keeping my promise and knew damn well that as soon as she left later that day, I'd start on a gallon of wine with dinner.

But for some reason I didn't. Maybe because I had enough of a conscience to at least try to honor my promise, but I doubt it. It felt more like a game. If she could do it, then I could, too. I didn't want to be bested. Whatever the reason, for the first time in more than ten years, I didn't have a drink. I'm sure it felt awful, but I don't remember. I'm sure I was scared and awake half the night, but I don't remember that either. What I do remember is what it was like to get up the next morning without a hangover for the first time in my adult life. I was giddy with joy, incredulous at the miracle of it. Maybe I wasn't an alcoholic after all. Maybe I could control this better than I thought. I didn't know I could go a whole night without drinking, but suddenly it became two nights, then three, and then a week.

Physically it felt wonderful. It was great to go to bed without seeing a spinning room and to wake up without immediately needing to vomit. It was nice to talk on the phone at night without slurring my words or to worry whether or not I would fall off the stool at the kitchen counter. It was a relief to jog with Bear in the morning and not feel that my heart was going to explode in my chest. I felt free of something enormous: an invisible force that had been controlling my life.

It wasn't all bliss. There were the wonderful mornings free of headaches and nausea, but then there was the rest of the day, after I'd finished my run with Bear and I'd head downstairs after my shower to figure out what to do with the rest of my life. There seemed to be a giant disconnect between what I wanted and what I was capable of—who I was and who I wanted to be. What I wanted was meaningful work, a few friends, a nice man, and some inner peace. None of it seemed within my reach. It was like trying to figure out infinity. After a few minutes, I just felt scared and agoraphobic, so what was the point? Infinity was for other people, people who could make sense of it.

I had worked once. I had taught high school English in Boston, followed by a stint as a department manager in a ski company. I'd had a few friends. I'd had a not-so-great boyfriend for a few years followed by the not-so-great husband. But the point is I had tried. I'd been in the game. I'd even had inner peace, which kicked in sometime around the second or third drink and lasted until what I referred to for years, quaintly, as "falling asleep."

But that was before I accidentally became sober and discovered that the very thing destroying my life had also helped make it possible because it quelled anxiety; the conundrum of alcohol. I could go upstairs after the morning jog and sit in the yellow chair in the living room facing the pond, the fields, and a mountain called High Point with a copy of *The Complete Works of Jane Austen* in my lap, and that was about it. That's what my day looked like. I'd lived in Olivebridge for a month, and the only person whose company I wanted to keep was a woman who'd been dead for a hundred sixty years.

I hadn't been aware of how much time drinking took up. It wasn't until after I stopped that I realized I had always either anticipated a drink or I had one. Although I had looked busy doing other things on any given day, the true centerpiece of my life was alcohol. Whatever I did, whether it was work-related, social, or even equine, it was just a way to pass the time until I could drink. Ordinarily, I drank only at night, but how I loved an excuse to drink during the day: Fourth of July picnics, business lunches, birthday parties. Any place drinks were offered, including mimosas at breakfast, I was more than happy to accept.

Suddenly, now I had a lot of time on my hands, and I had no idea what to do with it. It had been so long since I'd done anything at night that didn't involve drinking, I couldn't imagine what people did. Certainly I couldn't imagine what they did that was any fun. Movies? Concerts? Lectures? Surely people didn't do those things *sober*?

I never had and couldn't picture it now. I'd always been shy and self-conscious (nobody who met me when I was drinking would *ever* have known this), but when I became sober, those qualities intensified. The most overused word in my vocabulary, spoken or unspoken, was *overwhelmed*. Everything felt overwhelming: anything related to my divorce or finances, going to dinner with a friend, going to a party, meeting and talking to a neighbor while walking my dog, talking to anyone on the phone who asked how I was doing. Since I'd always kept my drinking a secret, how could I share the extraordinary news that I'd stopped? How could I tell anyone I felt *overwhelmed*?

A month later, while I was still euphoric with the newness of my sobriety, my lawyer called to tell me that my husband was willing to return Georgia. Nikka and Thunder had already gone back to Nikka's original owner, which didn't surprise me, but I would have my horse! I wasn't sure why he had changed his mind, why after nearly a year of expensive haggling, he had suddenly written the address of the farm where he had "hidden" her on the back of a dry-cleaning receipt and sent it to my lawyer. It was before we'd reached a final settlement, though it looked as though my husband was going to get most of what he wanted. Still, his concession seemed out of character, and I didn't trust it. What if I went to pick her up and she wasn't there? What if it was just a ruse to lure me someplace far away where he could hurt me? Even with all the assurances from my husband's lawyer and my own, I didn't feel safe letting my husband know where I was, not even for the few minutes it would take to load Georgia into a trailer.

I didn't go. Instead, Tim and his physically strongest

friend volunteered to drive a rented horse trailer six hours to the farm in northern Vermont where my husband had stashed Georgia. They agreed to call when they had safely loaded her and to make the roundtrip in one day. Two days after my lawyer received the dry-cleaning receipt, Tim and his friend pulled out of my driveway in Olivebridge on a May dawn to fetch my girl.

I could barely stand the tension of waiting, and after jogging with Bear, I sat near the phone for the rest of the morning and into the afternoon, twirling my hair into knots while trying to read Jane Austen. When the phone rang at two-thirty, I nearly fell out of my chair with the shock.

We have her! Tim shouted over the background of cars roaring down a nearby highway. *We let her out at this rest area to stretch, and she ran away, but we caught her and everything's good now. It was actually pretty funny.*

Funny? I was horrified. I pictured Georgia running onto the highway and being hit by a tractor-trailer. I pictured how frightened she must have been to walk out of a trailer and onto a patch of grass, next to a bunch of parked cars where people were coming and going from restrooms carrying strange objects, like babies or small dogs, that could terrify a horse. I pictured how she would flare her nostrils and cock her tail before yanking her lead line out of Tim's grip to bolt as far away as she could get.

It's not funny! I shouted back. *Don't let her out again!*

Okay, okay, he said. *I told you we got her back, and we're all set to go. We should be there before dark.*

My heart was still racing when I hung up. I should have gone with them. Tim obviously knew nothing about horses. Letting any horse out on a highway rest stop was dangerous and stupid, but Georgia was only four and still learning what it meant to live in a world that belonged to humans. As far as I know, she'd never seen a baby or watched someone run with a dog on a leash. There would be dozens of new sights and sounds at a rest area that could panic a young horse. It never occurred to me I needed to tell Tim that. It seemed like common sense to me.

Four hours later, Georgia walked off the trailer and trotted into the pasture of her new, much smaller farm, a farm with no barn and no fencing other than stone walls I wasn't one hundred percent sure were horse-proof. I counted on the richness of the grass to keep her content enough not to wander until I had time to build fences. I hadn't wanted to spend the money on building any until I knew for sure I was going to have her back. I hung on the newly erected gate with tears of joy as I watched her canter around the perimeter of the field, stretching her legs after the long ride. I couldn't tell if she was glad to see me or if she even remembered me. As for my part, there couldn't have been any doubt in her mind that whatever her status had been for the past year, here she was now a celebrity. She wasn't just welcomed on a red carpet, she would *live* on a red carpet, beginning with the one I unrolled on the cement floor in the garage, her temporary barn while the permanent one was being built.

Like a paparazzo, I took a picture of her in her garage-barn on a hot day in May. She looked particularly fetching peering out from the cool, bug-free space with the garden rake, the jumper cables, and the spare drive belt for the lawn mower hanging next to her on the wall. I had zigzagged a clothesline across the entrance, reinforced by a freestanding sawhorse, all of it ridiculously ineffective if she had expressed the slightest interest in breaking out. But she hadn't; instead she had lowered her head to busy herself with the hay heaped on her red carpet.

The unexpected return of Georgia had given me a surge of new hope about what was possible, how life could change for the better in an instant. I stopped feeling so overwhelmed and started feeling more in control. Maybe I could change, too. The first morning I rode her after her return, I was giddy with joy, a feeling so unfamiliar to me I thought I was cracking up. How else could I explain the chatter and laughter on the trail with her when I was all by myself? Georgia was back. My life could begin. I didn't know how, I just knew it could. It could begin with Georgia herself — grooming her, feeding her, riding her, finding a vet and a farrier. Suddenly it wasn't just me and Jane Austen anymore. I would need a barn and people to build it. I would need hay and fencing and tools. My life had a starting point, a new purpose, a horse around whom I could build something. It wasn't about me anymore. It was about Georgia and building a home together.

With Bear, I had kept to the road in front of the house for our jogs and to the nearby fields and woods for our walks. But with Georgia, I felt braver and began to go farther. Every morning we explored the trails and old logging roads that wound for miles behind the house, some across private land and others across Catskill State Park. I never knew which it was and hoped if I was caught trespassing, the owners would be as forgiving as owners in the Adirondacks had been. But that first month I didn't run into anyone, and it was easy to imagine we were the only creatures on earth. It gave me time to get to know my horse again, to remember all the reasons I had fallen in love with her in the first place — that big heart, her eagerness for the trail, her great stamina, and, of course, her beauty.

Each day's ride strengthened our bond and added to the feeling that with Georgia I had indeed found my home. When I looked out the living-room window and saw her grazing in the back pasture, a surge of warmth came over me as though some ancient wrong had finally been righted, as though I was back to a decades-old crossroad where my life had turned in the wrong direction but now, for the first time since I was five, I had a chance to start the journey over again. I had a home now, safe from alcohol and violence and filled with the love of a horse and a dog. It was a start.

{CHAPTER 4}

I WAS COMPLETELY LOST. I'd been riding for so long I could feel a blister on my bottom, so I tilted sideways in the saddle to shift my weight off the sore. The imbalance annoyed Georgia, and she fussed and bucked along the trail, probably tired and hungry, too, from this unintentional marathon. We'd been riding for five hours, since eight o'clock that morning, when I'd headed straight through the fields behind my new house and into the woods of the Catskill Mountains. I didn't know if we were now riding on private or state land, if we'd gone in circles or a straight line, or if we'd have to spend the night together huddled in the dark.

It was easy to feel sorry for myself, something I'd been doing on and off for the past month. I justified it with a long list of reasons: I was lonely; I was scared; I was almost broke; I was unemployed; I had repeatedly exercised bad judgment — for example, moving to a house that didn't have a barn or any fencing whatsoever but buying it anyway because it had beautiful old stone walls dividing its open fields and a pond for Bear. And I couldn't drink away my self-pity because I was no longer comforting myself with a gallon of wine every night.

I'd lived in the new house for six months but had brought Georgia there only a few weeks earlier. Of all the things I'd lost in the divorce — the house, most of my money, Nikka, Thunder, the dream of living in the Adirondacks — only the loss of Georgia had seemed unbearable. When I thought about my divorce, when years later someone would ask what it was like, how I had handled it, I would remember driving in my car and crying when I passed a field or a dirt road, even the open space of a school playground, anywhere I could possibly ride a horse. My husband knew that of all the things he could have taken from me, holding on to Georgia would hurt me the most.

Now, a few weeks after her miraculous return, we found ourselves tired and lost on our morning ride, remembering the garage-barn and the rest of the house fondly. If only I could have found it. Bear was with us, stopping to lie down at every opportunity, hours earlier having lost interest in the myriad new smells available to him in every direction. He kept to Georgia's slipstream, so close that her tail sometimes draped across his back.

I suspected Georgia remembered Bear, a harmless companion from her other life, someone she had occasionally chased across the pasture just for the fun of it, someone she had kicked once, somersaulting him into the air before he had landed at my feet whimpering. She was teaching me that you could be crazy angry and in love at the same time. She was teaching me it was pointless to hit. What seemed to work was to grab her halter, and with my face in hers, say in my meanest Mommy voice, *No more kicking!* For good measure I'd jerk her halter a few times, carefully searching the giant, beautifully fringed eye for signs of comprehension or remorse or fear. Maybe I was just looking in the wrong eye. Maybe the one on the other side of her face was full of self-incrimination and apology. Maybe I was still looking for answers in all the wrong places.

Nevertheless, her behavior had improved. The kicking stopped, and by the time she arrived in Olivebridge, she was almost five, an age by which most horses have learned the basics of acceptable social behavior, particularly as it applies to barn, pasture, and trail decorum. Bear was safe at her heel, maybe even welcome in this new world with no other horse yet for a companion. I suspected Georgia was lonely, and Bear was better than nothing.

After five hours of riding, the last three spent in growing alarm, I found it hard to recall the mood I'd been in earlier that day. Euphoria? Incredulity? Relief? Pride? I was sober. Rather, I had been sober the night before, one of more than a month of such nights that had produced the unexpected benefit of waking up without feeling nauseated, disoriented, anxious, and full of enough shame and remorse for a dozen Georgias.

The most extraordinary thing about alcoholism is the way it feels when it's over, when you're released from the

urge to drink in the first place. I hadn't known that freedom in a long time. I hadn't thought I would ever know it
again. But there I was, just over a month into not drinking
and reinventing morning. I was thirty-three.

To someone who must drink, to a person who cannot
imagine talking to a stranger, attending a social event,
being intimate with a lover, or living through the day
without counting the hours until 5 P.M., *not* drinking is the
unthinkable choice. The question for most alcoholics is
not how to stop drinking, but rather how to drink without
the negative consequences, how to drink smarter. When
that failed, when the drinking grew more frequent and the
consequences much worse, I told myself I knew plenty of
people who drank more. And it was true. I sought them
out. I embedded myself in a drinking culture, where the
people and places around me venerated drinking. They
were easy to find; whole industries were built around
drinking, entire lives.

Deciding not to drink anymore meant *un*-embedding
myself. It meant giving up the people, places, and things
I had surrounded myself with to support a drinking lifestyle that had been years in the making. It meant leaving
good friends and deciding to quit the ski business, an industry that no longer was a wise or safe choice for me,
with its endless parties always revolving around alcohol.
It meant getting rid of a kitchen full of drinking accoutre-
ments — the glasses, the wine cooler, the fancy corkscrew
collection, all the wine and liquor, and the pretty colored
bottles I kept to make my drinking friends happy. It meant
leaving one world where I knew how to get by and enter-
ing a new one where I didn't have a clue.

More difficult than anything, the reason so many people

ultimately never stop drinking, is the necessity of exchanging one identity for another. I knew who I was as a drinker. That identity, the confident, friendly, easygoing woman, might have been mostly a myth, but as long as I kept drinking, I wouldn't have to face that. But when the wine stopped flowing, there I was — someone I didn't know, someone full of nameless insecurities and fears with a one-size-fits-all coping skill: alcohol.

The truth was, I'd been hiding for years, long before alcohol had added another layer to the mask I wore. I had started hiding my real self when I'd gone to live with my grandmother. I remember realizing, within minutes of living with her, that it wasn't safe to tell her anything — whether I was or wasn't hungry, scared or not scared, or whether I did or didn't miss my mother and father. I knew that if I didn't want to be hurt in that house, I had to be quiet. I learned to smile and agree with everything anyone said no matter what I thought. That kind of blind compliance became even more necessary when at the age of nine, after a year of living with my aunt and uncle in Boston, my grandmother moved me again, this time to live with my mother's father in Baltimore and his second wife, Jean. There, I went from hiding who I was to forgetting who I was. By then it had been so long since I'd disappeared behind the smile, I didn't remember I had a choice. Even my fifth-grade math teacher had sent a note home to my grandfather saying, *Susie doesn't seem to take school seriously. When told she was failing math, she smiled.* Since becoming sober, whenever I felt lost and scared, I'd remind myself what it had been like in Baltimore. I'd remember the four most difficult years of my life.

· ı ·

I am wearing a summer dress and sneakers on the August afternoon when I meet my grandfather and his wife and daughter at a restaurant halfway between New York and Baltimore. Franz, my grandmother's chauffeur, has driven my grandmother and me here because I am going to live with my mother's father, his much younger second wife, and their adopted daughter. I have met them once before, when I was five, and played in a round plastic pool on a hot day in their front yard in Baltimore.

My grandfather wears tortoise-shell glasses and talks with a southern accent. His wife, Jean, was his secretary before they married. She grew up in the Bronx, but she doesn't sound like a Bronx native. She is short and pretty and calls my grandmother Eleanor. Their daughter, Nancy, has long blond hair and is wearing shorts and pointy-toed shoes my grandmother would have thrown in the trash.

I feel shy and ugly in Nancy's presence. She is eleven years old and the prettiest girl I've ever seen. I'm nine, with a pale round face and short brown curly hair. When I see myself in a mirror, I look away. Nancy and I sip milk shakes at the counter while the adults talk at a table across the room. Nancy isn't friendly. *Why do you have to come here?* she asks. She means to Baltimore, to live in her house and go to her school.

I don't know, I say. And it's the truth. Last year, I lived with my aunt and uncle and their three daughters in a town near Boston. Before that I lived with my grandmother, going back and forth between her houses in New York and South Carolina. Before that I don't remember, but it wasn't like this. Before that I belonged somewhere.

Maybe you won't stay, Nancy says, stirring her milk shake with the kind of long white fingers you see in magazines.

Maybe, I say with a shrug, desperate for her to like me. *Maybe it's just for a few weeks.*

Don't be stupid, she says. *Your uniforms are hanging in the closet. But maybe you'll leave in the spring.*

She's referring to the uniform we have to wear to school, a private, all-girls' day school that won't put up with my shenanigans, Grandmother has told me. She means the Ds and Fs all over my report card, the comments that say I'm a daydreamer, a lazy student, a careless worker.

A few hours later I walk into a big stone house with Oriental rugs and formal furniture my grandmother would have called fussy. On the walls are large oil paintings of somber-looking men and women in carved gold frames; Grandmother would have shaken her head in disgust. Everywhere I look there is silver and china. I wonder if my grandmother would have sent me to live here if she had seen the house first. *Dreadful,* she would have said. *Everything is dreadful.* Grandmother likes modern art: Calder mobiles, Noguchi tables, and large bright tapestries from Poland. Her houses are sunny and quiet and cannot be seen from the road. Grandfather's house is on a busy street with other big houses and small yards because it is practically in downtown Baltimore.

The furniture in my room is white with gold trim, and everything matches: the twin beds with the night table between them, the dressing table, the bureau, and the little desk with the fold-out top. On the bureau, crystal candelabras stand at either side of the mirror. The French doors are framed by heavy, floor-length curtains. In the closet hang five royal blue cotton dresses with white collars and cuffs. They're ugly, but not as ugly as the clothes my grandmother makes me wear.

I sit on the edge of the bed holding a stuffed animal in each arm: my bear, Toboe, and his best friend, a seal named Sealy. I can't imagine them sleeping in this room. The beds are covered in slippery, pale green spreads that look like something you'd use to make a ball gown. All the lampshades are white and lacy.

I don't know what to do or where to go. Nancy's room is next to mine, but as soon as we arrive, she goes to her room and slams the door. Jean brought me upstairs and told me to unpack my suitcase.

No shoes on the bed, she says when she leaves.

Later, Jean shows me where the silverware is and asks me to set the table for dinner. As Nancy and I carry food from the kitchen to the dining room, we pass through the pantry, which has a large copper-lined sink full of liquor bottles. My grandfather leans against the sink with a drink in his hand. He is the only one who is smiling, the only one who sounds happy.

There is a big sterling-silver rooster in the middle of the dining room table, and when all four of us are settled in our chairs, my grandfather smiles and says to me, *How do you like my cock?*

My face burns and I stare at my plate. It sounds like a question he has asked before, a standard joke to anyone who is eating dinner there for the first time, but I can't bear to look at him. Nancy rolls her eyes. Jean hisses something to him under her breath, but I can't see her face across the table because the rooster is in the way. The cock. Suddenly Nancy and Grandfather are reaching for my hands, and we're all holding hands around the table when Jean says, *Susie, why don't you say grace?*

I've never said grace. My grandmother doesn't believe

in God. I don't know what my aunt and uncle believe, but we didn't go to church. *I don't know any,* I say.

Good grief, Nancy says, rolling her eyes again. *I'll do it.*

Grandfather leaves twice during dinner to pour himself another drink, and by the time dessert comes, his face is red and his eyes never look higher than my neck.

Welcome tobalimore, Susie, isjus trific you're withis.

See what you've done, Nancy says to me and leaves the table without touching her dessert. I can hear her footsteps up the stairs, and a second later a door slams.

Jean stands up and throws her napkin at my grandfather. It hits his face before it falls onto his dessert plate. *I don't have to take this crap,* she says and walks out. I hear the front door slam, and a few minutes later the car roars down the driveway.

Boy, we sure cleared 'em out, dint we, ole Susie-Q, my grandfather says, grinning at my neck. He pushes himself out of the chair and on unsteady feet makes his way to the pantry.

As soon as his back is turned, I leave the table and run up the stairs to my room. It is too early to go to sleep, but I take off the slippery spread and climb into bed with Toboe and Sealy and my favorite book, *Born Free.* I look at the pictures of the rescued lion, Elsa, riding on top of the car and sleeping next to the author on a cot. As soon as I am eighteen, I decide, I will go to Africa. I will live in a tent like Joy Adamson's and save lions and elephants from poachers. I worry about the tsetse flies that make you sleepy and the snakes that can swallow a baby zebra whole, but Joy Adamson looks so beautiful with her blond hair and khaki safari outfit that it can't be that bad. It can't be as bad as here.

I'm put in the dumb section at school, but I still get bad grades on all my papers and tests. I have to stay after school for extra help, and a tutor even comes to the house sometimes, but none of it works. I'm the worst student in the class. I have only one friend, and her name is Beth. She's one of the few girls who will talk to me, so we play jacks together during recess and after lunch. Nancy is two classes ahead of me, but when she sees me in the hall, she crosses to the other side and looks away. She is one of the popular girls, and they are always laughing.

On Saturday mornings I stand at the fence and watch Nancy take her riding lesson. She is allergic to horses and doesn't want to ride, but Jean makes her do this. *It is like dance school and piano lessons and curtsying when you meet a stranger. It's what young ladies do,* Jean says.

For the first time in my life I am not allowed to ride because of my bad grades, so I stand at the fence with a racing heart and hope the riding instructor will save me from this nightmare by telling me to saddle up and join the class. She doesn't, and week after week I watch Nancy grudgingly take her lesson, shocked to see that she never learns anything about horses. She never connects to her horse because she doesn't understand her horse at all, that it is a being, an entity, a whole separate personality with likes and dislikes, good days and bad days and everything else. It is only missing the ability to speak. But I know how a horse talks. It's all there in the eyes, the angle of the head, the posture, the gait, and how she carries her tail. It will tell you who a horse is, what she thinks of you, what she thinks of what you're doing, and what she wants. Nancy doesn't see any of this. She rides her horse like a bike, something without thought or feeling. They go around and around the ring, but they're like two strangers on a sidewalk. They're walking in the same direction, but they're not together.

I know what Nancy's horse feels. It has been a long time since anyone has asked me what I think or feel. It has been a long time since I've been seen, so long that I'm no longer myself. I can feel the memory of who I once was slipping away, going into hiding until some time or place in the future when it will be safe to come out. Maybe Nancy's horse feels the same way. She is just waiting for the moment when somewhere, somehow she can be herself without having her mouth jerked, her sides kicked, or her back pounded.

My moment will come when I am eighteen. I am certain of this and even plan it. It will be far away from Baltimore; Rye, New York; and Boston. It will be far away from everyone I ever knew. When people ask me what I want to be when I grow up, sometimes I say a vet, and sometimes I say a writer, and sometimes I say I don't know. I never say I want to be myself, but I think it.

Nancy is always having her picture taken. Once it was someone from the newspaper who took pictures of her making fudge in the kitchen after school while she was still wearing her uniform. He posed her at the stove stirring the chocolate, only the pot was empty and Nancy never eats fudge. One time she had her picture taken walking her black poodle, Petey, and another time when she was dancing with someone at dancing school. All of them end up in the society section of the newspaper. My picture is never taken, and I try not to think about why.

Jean and Nancy are hitters. They don't hit each other, but they hit me. Sometimes Jean hits me with her hand and sometimes she uses a belt. I never know when it's going to happen, so I stay in my room as much as possible. Once a week the whole family sits together and watches the *Mitch Miller Show* on television while we eat cheesecake. I don't like Mitch Miller or cheesecake, but I do it anyway because I don't want to get hit.

Sometimes, after Jean hits me, I leave the house without telling her and go to see Granny Blake. She used to be Granny Harrison before she married her second husband, who's now dead. It's about a thirty-minute walk to my great-grandmother's apartment, and by the time I get there I've stopped crying and composed myself enough to pretend that everything's fine. She answers the door, smoking, and I follow her down the hall to the living room, where there are views from every window of the city far below. She goes to the kitchen and brings back a tin of butter cookies, which I eat while she smokes one cigarette after another. She's almost eighty and wears her long white hair in a messy knot on top of her head. She is still thin and likes to wear black silk dresses and high heels. My grandfather resents his mother because she was frequently absent when he was growing up. She was a foreign correspondent for the *Baltimore Sun* and spent most of her time traveling around the world, leaving my grandfather in the care of a governess. Once, when she was arrested in Russia for spying and sent to the Lubyanka Prison, she left him for two years in a Swiss boarding school. Jean resents her because she won't lend Jean her diamond jewelry. Granny Blake says Jean is nothing but a social climber.

Mostly Granny Blake tells me stories about the places she's been, but sometimes she picks up the newspaper to see what movie is playing nearby, and if it's one that seems OK, she puts on her big fur coat, and off we go. No matter what the movie is, she falls asleep, sometimes with a lit cigarette dangling from her fingers, which I remove as carefully as possible, drop on the floor, and put out with my shoe. When the movie is over, I wake her up, and we walk to an ice cream parlor with a black-and-white-checkered marble floor and drink Coke floats with strawberry ice cream at the counter. She barely touches hers, but when I'm finished, we walk back to her apartment and she calls Jean to let her know where I am. She shuts the door while she's on the phone so I can't hear what she's saying, but I can tell by the tone of her voice that she's angry. After these visits, Jean stops hitting me for a while.

I'm afraid if I tell anyone that Jean hits or that Grandfather is drunk every night, it will only make things worse. The headmistress of the school calls me into her office a few months after school has begun to ask if everything is OK. She wants to know why I am having trouble in school. She wants to know why I am so dumb.

Are you happy? she asks, flipping through papers on her desk, looking for something. My heart races, and I can feel the pressure of tears as I consider how to answer her. Maybe if she looks at me, maybe if just once she looks up from her desk and stops signing things and shifting folders around, I will be able to tell her the truth. But she never looks up except to frown at me once. *Did you hear the question?* she asks, glancing at her watch.

Weeks later I'm in a psychologist's office. Jean has driven me here to find out if I'm crazy on top of being dumb. The psychologist takes me to a little room with a desk and gives me a bunch of written questions. *Answer them all even if you don't know the answer,* he says, shutting the door as he leaves.

The very first question makes me almost dizzy with confusion.

Do you love your parents?

For a few minutes I try to figure out whom he means. My own mother and father, whom I hardly remember? Grandmother Richards? My aunt and uncle in Boston, where I lived for a year before I was sent to Baltimore? Jean and Grandfather? Then I realize it doesn't matter because there's only one answer. One answer if I don't want to get hit.

Yes, I write, pressing so hard I break the tip off the pencil.

Later, I sit in a chair across from his desk and watch as he flips through the pages of my answers. Before he says a single word to me, the phone on his desk rings and he answers it. He swivels in his chair so his back is turned to me while he talks. He talks for so long I begin to feel angry. Twenty minutes goes by, thirty, forty-five. I am nine years old, but I know that what he is doing is wrong. I know he is supposed to talk to me and not to whoever is on the phone. When an hour has passed, he swivels back to face me as he hangs up. He smiles and says he is sorry. I am glad I have lied on the questions. I will never tell him anything.

It is a Saturday in late spring, and Jean, Grandfather, Nancy, and I are sitting around the wrought iron table on the patio in the backyard. Jean has called a "family" meeting, which is what she does when a problem is too big to be solved by just hitting someone. The last time she called a meeting, it was to tell Nancy that she didn't approve of the boy Nancy danced with at dance school. Nancy was mad and told her mother she could dance with whomever she wanted. Grandfather agreed, and Jean stood up to leave the meeting so fast she knocked over her chair. I am in awe that Nancy is not afraid of her mother.

I am less nervous than usual about this meeting because school is almost over, and I'll be leaving in a few days to spend two months at the same camp in the Adirondacks I've been going to every summer since I was five years old. It is a place where my best friend, Sidney, and I will spend almost every waking moment on horses. I will shower only when forced to, and at night I will fall asleep whispering and giggling with my tent mates. When I'm at camp I am as close to being myself as I can be because I'm around horses and donkeys and a whole barnyard full of animals. Nobody there thinks I am dumb.

Grandfather glances at his watch because what he really wants to do is play golf. When he isn't drinking, he hardly has anything to say. Jean stares at the table with her arms folded across her chest, and Nancy studies a strand of hair, pinching off split ends. I can tell that none of them wants to be here, which means this meeting is about me. I am filled with dread before anyone says a word. I'm afraid Jean is going to say I can't go to camp, that I will have to spend the summer in Baltimore with them.

We have tried everything, Jean begins, lifting her eyes from the table and looking right at me, *but school says you will probably fail most of your subjects. We've decided you should stay back. You'll have to repeat the grade.*

I feel myself recoil as if she has hit me. Stay back? Walk into the same classroom — only with the younger kids from the grade behind me — where everyone will know I have failed? Where I will have to endure the glances and snickers of my former classmates when I bump into them in the hall? Nancy is already snickering, pinching split ends and giggling as if she is watching me trip on the sidewalk. Grandfather shakes his head, smiling, and pushes his chair back to stand up. *Just think, Susie-Q, this time 'round you'll get all As,* he says, patting me on the shoulder. *I have a ten o'clock tee,* he says to Jean and rushes into the house.

I start to cry, filled with a feeling I can't identify. I know I'm ashamed that I still get long division wrong and history dates mixed up and make the same spelling errors over and over again. I'm ashamed I don't have more friends, and that no matter what I do, Nancy doesn't like me. I'm ashamed that when I'm not wearing my uniform, I have to wear ugly clothes and shoes I never would have chosen, and I'm ashamed I'm not pretty. But mostly I'm ashamed that I don't have parents or anyone who cares one bit about me.

And then suddenly I know what I'm feeling. It scares me so much I stop crying because it's the first time I've ever felt it. It's hate. I am filled with hate. I hate Jean and Nancy and Grandfather and failing school and living in Baltimore and standing at the fence watching Nancy ride and never having my picture taken and being alone in my room for hours and no one ever coming to ask what I'm doing or if I'm lonely. I hate being hit. I hate being scared. I hate being unloved.

But I hate hating. It feels like in an instant I've gone from being one kind of person to being another, as though suddenly I've become mean, someone who kicks a dog or jerks a horse. I feel poisoned. I look at Jean and Nancy, two people who have never uttered a single kind word to me, and I am helpless against the hatred I feel for them. It is impossible to express. For one thing I'm not brave enough, and for another it is beyond words. I want them to suffer. I want them to die. I want them to clutch their sides howling and die like the Wicked Witch in *The Wizard of Oz,* where nothing will remain but two smoldering heaps of clothes.

Two months later, in the middle of July, I'm dressed in dirty riding clothes eating lunch in the dining room at Camp Treetops. It is my turn to wait on tables, and I walk back and forth from the kitchen bringing food and clearing plates. The room is filled with the chatter of eighty campers. In the middle of lunch, a counselor comes to my table and says, *Your grandmother Harrison called to say she is coming to visit you this afternoon.*

I'm confused. I have two Grandmother Harrisons. One is my mother's mother, the one Grandfather divorced who lives in Switzerland but has a summer house in Maine. I haven't seen her since I was a baby and have no memory of her. The other one is Jean. *Which one?* I ask.

I'm sorry, the counselor says with a shrug, *I don't know.*

It is impossible to imagine either one coming to visit me, so impossible that I don't believe for a minute that it will happen. One doesn't know me, and the other hates me.

After lunch I walk to the barn with my best friend, Sidney, and two other girls to spend the afternoon bringing in hay. We hop in the back of the old hay truck with the wobbly wooden sides, gripping the top of the cab and letting our hair blow wild in the wind. The truck bounces down a dirt road and then turns into a fifty-acre hay field scattered with a thousand fresh bales. The open space and the sweet smell of cut hay is intoxicating, and we jump out of the truck running and laughing across the field before we get down to the business of throwing the bales into the back of the truck to be stacked by the two male counselors we are helping. I love haying so much that I soon forget about the possibility of a visitor. The work is hard and physical, and within minutes our arms have angry red welts where we have been scratched by hay. None of us minds. On the contrary, we view the marks as a symbol of our status as the four best riders in camp. We are the horsiest, the ones counselors and campers alike watch with admiration whenever we are in the saddle. We are allowed to take our horses out and ride alone anywhere. We are trusted.

It takes two hours and almost a hundred bales to fill the truck, and by the time we do, we are goofy with exhaustion. The bales are tied down with rope, and then we are allowed to climb to the top to ride back to camp while holding on to the wooden sides. The afternoon floods the field in a warm yellow light, and all around us are the high peaks of the Adirondacks, many of which we have climbed. The truck bounces across the pasture, rocking this way and that under the weight of the hay, and we scream with delight every time it tilts. All the way back to camp we hoot and holler, letting the truck throw us around on top of the bales, colliding into one another at every bump in the road.

As we pull into the barnyard, the four of us are lying on our backs with our heads dangling down the back end of the truck, pretending we are about to fall out. We are laughing so hard, we can hardly talk, and that is when I see Jean and Grandfather standing next to their parked car, waiting for me. I sit up quickly, self-conscious because I suddenly realize that I have never laughed in their presence. They have never seen me with friends. They don't know the person who goes to this camp. Whoever that person is disappears in their presence. In an instant, I feel myself grow quiet and tight. I am horrified that they have caught me laughing. I am horrified that they have glimpsed even a moment of who I really am. I am horrified that they are here.

I climb down from the truck and walk across the dusty barnyard toward their car. No one hugs, but I smile and say hello. I can feel the hate coming back as soon as I'm near them. My grandfather pats my shoulder and makes a joke about seeing me almost fall out of the truck. Jean wrinkles her nose at my dirty clothes and says I've grown. They look all wrong standing next to the big gray barn, surrounded by wandering chickens and braying donkeys at the paddock fence. My grandfather is wearing a yellow sweater vest over a blue button-down shirt and a striped tie. Jean is wearing a white sleeveless shirt with a diamond circle pin and pink Bermuda shorts with matching flats. They look like they are on their way to a party in someone's backyard.

Jean crosses her arms and looks around with pinched lips. She doesn't know that this barn, with its rusty overhead door tracks and its missing or rotten clapboards, is beautiful. She doesn't think the donkeys are irresistibly cute or that a chicken is a nice thing to hug. She doesn't think the big pile of manure behind the barn is a comforting smell. She doesn't think this is heaven. She doesn't know that this is the only place where pieces of who I really am begin to wake up and come back to life.

Grandfather shoves his hands in the pockets of his gray slacks and says, *Well, Susie-Q, here you are at camp. Imagine that.* He hardly knows what to say without a drink in his hand, but even if he had one, he'd say the same thing, only louder. I don't know what to say to him either. I don't know what to say to either of them.

One of the counselors comes over and introduces himself. He asks where they're from and if they've had a nice drive. Then he tells them what a big help I am around the barn. *She's a hard worker,* he says and gives my shoulders a squeeze. It is the first time an adult has said something nice about me in front of them. I wonder if they think he is lying. Still, it feels really good, so good that it gives me enough courage not to be friendly. I don't care if they don't like this barn. I don't care if they don't like me. *Why don't you show them around camp?* the counselor suggests.

I get in the back seat of their car, and we drive down the long dirt road past the organic vegetable garden where I weed a row of beets once a week, but I don't tell them that. I don't tell them about eating the strawberries we pick to make preserves, and I don't tell them about learning to eat nasturtiums in a salad. I don't tell them anything. When we get to the main part of camp, we park and get out of the car. I point to the hillside dotted with orange tents and tell them which one is mine. They can see everything else because we are standing on top of a hill and the lake and various buildings are in full view all around us. As we stand there looking, everyone who walks by says hello to me, and I almost burst with happiness that Jean and Grandfather see this. I feel beyond their reach here,

protected from them by this place and these people whom
I love.

Someone comes up behind me and yanks my hair. I
turn to see Sidney, who has walked back from the barn and
is on her way to the tent to change into her bathing suit.
She smiles hello at Jean and Grandfather and then says to
me, *There's only half an hour left to swim.* We swim together
every afternoon, usually after riding, when we have just
enough time before barn chores and dinner.

Go ahead, Grandfather says. *We just stopped on our way
back from visiting friends. Go ahead*, he says again. I know he
wants to leave to get a drink.

Yes, go, agrees Jean. *We have a long drive to our hotel.*

It seems too good to be true that they will leave less than
an hour after they have arrived. It seems like a miracle, and
I say nothing that will stop them.

See you in a month or so, Grandfather says, patting my
shoulder.

Standing on this hill next to Sidney with our horses
stalled in the barn down the road and looking at the lake
and the tents and the mountains all around us, it is impossible to believe this will ever have to end. It is impossible
to imagine living in Baltimore with those two people.

I watch their car disappear down the long dirt road
that will take them past the rows of vegetables, then past
the barn; when their trail of dust has settled and I know
they're gone for sure, I turn to Sidney, who knows how
much I hate them, and we scream with laughter. It is the
funniest thing ever that they showed up at all and funnier
still that they left so quickly. We race up the hill toward the
tent, pretending to be on our horses. We buck and kick,
but we don't fall off because we are good riders; we are the

best. By the time we get to the tent, our horses are panting and snorting, so we ride them in circles to settle them
down. It is hard because they are strong and spirited and
they want to run forever.

Hurry, Sidney says, dismounting first and running into
the tent to change.

Okay, I say, but my horse is still dancing, still circling the
tent breathless and eager, filled with hate and happiness
and ready to gallop across mountains. And I don't want to
stop her from going because that is just who she is.

Now, lost again, this time with Bear and Georgia in the
woods near Olivebridge, another accident saved us when
we stumbled onto the pasture where a woman was just
turning out a white Arab gelding. At the sight of us, her
horse had run the length of the pasture to sniff nose to
nose with Georgia across the top of the fence, both of
their necks stiff and arched with curiosity and, to my
embarrassment, hostility as Georgia squealed and struck
out with a front leg. She seemed incapable of meeting another animal without asserting her dominance. Once her
dominance was proclaimed, as long as everyone agreed to
her rules, she was OK—not friendly, just no longer lethal.
When the Arab didn't challenge her, she lost interest in
him and focused on trying to squeeze her fat head through
the bottom two fence boards to get at the grass on the
other side.

I pulled her head up and rode toward the woman waving
to us from the barnyard on the other side of the field.

You must be lost, she said with a laugh as we approached.

Bear dragged himself behind Georgia, and the three of

us came to a weary stop in front of the open doorway of her large gray barn, set less than twenty feet from a paved road. Although I was a lover of solitude and wilderness, never had I been so glad to see human and macadam in the same spot.

I'm Julie, she said, thrusting her hand upward.

I returned her handshake from the saddle, afraid that if I dismounted, I'd be too sore and too tired to remount.

Julie laughed again when I told her how long I'd been lost; she explained that my house was less than two miles from where we stood, a left and a right and we'd be there, just around a country corner. She said she knew I'd moved there six months ago and had always meant to stop by. When I looked surprised, she said she'd lived on this farm her whole life and knew everyone who came and went for miles around. With the exception of my immediate neighbor, whom I bought eggs from, I'd never met anyone on my road or any road near it. I'd felt invisible in my new house. It was me and Jane Austen, just the way I wanted it most of the time. Or did I? It felt nice talking to Julie, another woman about my age living alone on a farm with her horse. I didn't know much else about her, but it was enough that she was warm and friendly, that she had filled a feed bucket with water for Bear, and that she didn't hold Georgia's behavior toward her Arab against her.

She's gorgeous, she'd said of Georgia, the only acceptable observation I was willing to hear. Among other things, sobriety had revealed a couple of new character traits: a crippling shyness in almost any social situation and a protectiveness toward Georgia that seemed absurd, given Georgia's cocky persona.

You must be thirsty, too, Julie said to me, watching Bear

prostrate in front of the water bucket, his head half hidden inside, lapping loudly. *And I have just the thing.* She turned to walk to her car, parked just a few yards away with the back door still open, revealing several full grocery bags. I couldn't help but notice that the floor of the car was covered with empty beer cans. She reached inside one of the bags and pulled out a six-pack of beer. She stumbled a little as she walked back to me, freeing two cans from the plastic rings holding them together and tossing me one before I could say no. She popped the flip top on hers and drank the whole can in one long guzzle. She barely paused before freeing another can, and then, just before drinking it, she reached into her breast pocket and threw me a pack of cigarettes.

Help yourself, she said. *Looks like you could use one of these, too.*

I could have used one. Rather, I could have used both packs — all to myself, the beer and the cigarettes, two of life's staples, as necessary as, well, as necessary as beer and cigarettes, the Swiss Army knife of the addicted, the first aid kit of the lost. But that had been more than a month ago, another lifetime. Still, there I was, the new me, the sober, nonsmoking me, shaky at best in this new life flooded with a sometimes awful clarity.

I glanced at my potential new friend, realizing she was probably drinking her eighth or ninth beer of the afternoon with no sign of slowing down, and, of course, I recognized her. She was me: smiling and helpful, a neighbor who for six months had "meant" to stop by to welcome me but had never gotten around to it. I suspected somewhere in the back seat of her car was another six-pack, that one empty, enjoyed on the twenty-mile drive back from the grocery store. She was a drunk, her faltering gait more obvious now that I knew it for what it was. Even her friendliness seemed less authentic, filled with the gushing warmth of barstool intimacy. I knew her. I knew her so well. It made me sad hearing her say all the things I would have said, weaving to and fro on slightly unsteady feet, thinking no one would notice. She even had the beautiful horse, the tidy farm, the nice car, proof that all was well, that whoever lived here was in control of her life.

Of the two things she offered, it was the pack of cigarettes that was the hardest to return. As she reached to take them back, I leaned into the gray plume from her lit cigarette, hoping just by the proximity to recapture some of that elusive inner peace. That's what she seemed to offer, inner peace and friendship, two of the most important things on my list. But watching Julie with her bright smile and too loud laugh, I knew I couldn't get either from her. I knew I couldn't be her friend. And for the first time in a long time, I knew I was not that lost. Not anymore. With Georgia steady beneath me, with her strength throughout this uncertain ride, I knew Julie's way was no longer my way and that together, Georgia and I would follow a new path.

{CHAPTER 5}

A WEEK AFTER becoming lost in the woods, I
woke up early one morning, walked to the back pasture
to fetch Georgia for our morning ride, and discovered she
was gone. After a panicky search on foot with Bear, I realized she was nowhere to be found in the fields or woods
surrounding the house, and she was nowhere to be seen on
the road. Losing a horse is different from losing a dog. You
never see stray horses wandering along the side of the road
or roaming in herds in the back alleys of small towns. Not
in America. If a horse breaks out of the pasture, unless it's
an enamored stallion, it usually goes no farther than the
nearest bit of green grass, typically its own backyard just

a few feet from the knocked-down fence. Over the years, after Georgia's stable mates Hotshot and Tempo joined us, I'd wake up fairly regularly to find my three horses grazing just off the back deck of my house, fifty feet from the wrong side of the fence. At the sound of the sliding glass doors opening, they'd jerk their heads up from their binge on lawn grass, their equivalent of eating Ben and Jerry's ice cream, and with eyes wide and defiant, wait for the chase to begin.

Fortunately, I knew better than to run after three horses, especially when Georgia was in charge of their strategy. I could chase all day and never know the feel of a halter in my outstretched hand. Of course I learned this the hard way, the first time I'd discovered them sampling the birdseed next to the kitchen window one morning and walked up to Georgia thinking I'd just slip my hand through her halter and we'd have a civilized stroll together back to the barn, with the other two following.

There had been signs of my flawed thinking from the moment Georgia's eyes met mine over the little copper roof of the newly hung feeder. The first clue alone should have stopped me dead in my tracks; the sudden cocking of her tail was as clear as the sweep of a flag at the start of the Indy 500. Maybe I hadn't had my coffee yet, or maybe I just counted on the solidity of our relationship and that we both understood that I knew best. But somehow I missed that important first clue, which was quickly followed by the second, *the look*. All horses do it. It is a throwback to when they were babies and everything in their world was new and scary and could possibly kill them, and so it required standing completely rigid with flared nostrils while looking crazed and demented at the sight of a rake, for example.

But when the adult Georgia gave me the look, it meant many things, none of which included the belief that her death was imminent. At the bird feeder that morning, it meant we weren't going to the barn together anytime soon. Sure enough, a few seconds later she was kicking and bucking herself across the lawn with Tempo and Hotshot in pursuit while the human trotted behind. Farther and farther behind.

After that, when I'd meet a horse on the lawn or anywhere else outside the pasture fence, I knew to ignore the cocked tail, the crazed eyes announcing as clear as spoken English, *I am going to jitterbug my way to New York City if I feel like it,* and with my head down, I would walk slowly and nonchalantly to the barn, where I would make a lot of noise in the feed room. Soon I would hear the sound of twelve hooves thundering across the pasture before skidding around the corner of the barn and clattering down the concrete center aisle to crowd in front of the feed-room door in anticipation of grain. Grain trumped grass, and apparently it even trumped being free.

But that morning in early June, only a week after Georgia had arrived from her farm in Vermont, I knew she had gone a lot farther than the backyard. She was young and tireless, and depending on what time she had either climbed or jumped over the steep rock wall that enclosed her pasture, she could be twenty miles away or more.

Bear had disappeared once, too. It was a few weeks after I moved to Olivebridge, but before I'd stopped drinking, just after New Year's Eve, which I had celebrated in the new house by getting drunk and falling down the spiral staircase. In the morning I woke up and couldn't find Bear for our first jog of the New Year. Instead of jogging, I drove around and posted notices on telephone poles within a three-mile radius of my house and on the bulletin board of the little deli where two country roads crossed before disappearing deeper into the Catskills.

On the sixth morning of his disappearance, I sat in the kitchen in my bathrobe, hung over, heartbroken, and weeping over the loss of my dog when I heard a muffled cry come from the cabinets under the counter. Bear had been locked in a cabinet for six days? I flew off the stool, filled with crazy hope that a one-hundred-twenty-pound dog would fit into one of the small cabinets that were already crammed with pots and pans and that he would have remained there quiet and content without food or water for six days before making a single sound. I looked in every cabinet anyway. Twice. I wasn't really surprised not to find a dog, but that meant I was in rougher shape than I thought. Auditory hallucinations are never a good sign. Had I finally drunk myself into insanity?

Maybe I was crazy to think I heard him in the cabinets, but the crying persisted. So after checking the cabinet under the bathroom sink down the hall, I did the first reasonable thing that morning and opened the front door. There was Bear, crying on the front porch the way he always did when he wanted to come in, only this time he'd been out for six days. Years later I learned that he had wandered to a house about half a mile away, and the owner, fearing the dog was abandoned, decided to keep him. On the sixth day, Bear jumped over her fence and walked home.

Losing Georgia was my first crisis since getting sober. Besides Tim, my sort of boyfriend in New Jersey, I didn't know a single person I could ask for help in finding her. I'd lived in Olivebridge for six months, and the only people I

knew to say hello to were the checkout girls at the grocery store and the vet who pulled a bunch of porcupine
quills out of Bear's face one afternoon. I don't know what
I did for all those months before Georgia arrived from Vermont. I must have stayed in touch with my brother and
a few friends in Boston, but what I remember the most
after unpacking and arranging my new house was reading,
walking through the woods near my property with Bear,
and drinking at night while wondering if I'd ever be able
to stop.

I'd lost contact with almost everyone I worked with in
the ski business, partly as a result of becoming sober and
partly because I didn't want anyone to tell my husband
where I had moved. I had an unlisted phone number,
which I gave out to almost no one; this was before the
advent of home computers and e-mail, so what I really did
those first months in Olivebridge was hide. I told myself I
was hiding from a violent man, which was only part of the
truth because the whole truth was that I was hiding from
everything. Whatever life skills I had once possessed such
as making friends or holding down a job seemed to have
vanished. I felt scared, vulnerable, and childish, as though
I had never been an adult with the responsibility of taking
care of myself in the first place.

Even riddled with anxiety as I often had been in the
past, I'd never before hidden away in a house. I'd never
felt like withdrawing from the whole world the way I did
when I moved to Olivebridge. I didn't understand what
had happened, why suddenly the thought of looking for
work and mingling with people and just being out in the
world filled me with such dread. Many years later I would
look back at the time just after my divorce and consider

that, coupled with being newly sober, I must have been suffering from posttraumatic shock after the violence of my marriage. It would be years before I stopped fearing I'd run into my husband. And even though I never did run into him, I couldn't stop looking over my shoulder until almost twenty years later when I found out he had died.

When Georgia disappeared, since there was no one to ask for help, I did the same thing I'd done with Bear; I posted signs with her picture and my phone number on telephone polls and on the bulletin board at the little deli at the crossroads. Nothing happened. Not a single phone call. How could a horse just vanish? I was sure she had been stolen. A horse rustler had come in the middle of the night, stolen my beautiful Morgan, and taken her to his hideout somewhere out of state where he would sell her for dog food or turn her into a rodeo bronco. He would already have discovered she was pretty good at bucking.

I drove around Olivebridge in tears, peering over back-yard fences and into the cobwebby doorways of old barns and tractor sheds. On a windy afternoon, three days after Georgia disappeared, I was less than three miles from my house when I passed a big red barn with the main doors rolled all the way back so you could see half the stalls inside. And there, in the end stall closest to the road, was Georgia's head bobbing impatiently over the stall door. The owner of the farm had found Georgia grazing in the town cemetery and knew that if she brought her back and put her in this particular stall, whoever owned the horse would eventually drive by and see her.

After a tearful reunion, I drove home, followed by the owner of the red barn, who then drove me back in her car with a bridle so I could ride Georgia home. I was curious to see where Georgia would go, if she knew or recognized where her home was, so I gave her no instruction for which way to turn when we reached the road. But not only did she know which way to turn, she knew all the turns in between, and she took us at a fast clip the whole way. I was thrilled to learn that she wanted to go home. But more than that, it was the first time I'd felt that this horse, whom I loved so much, was beginning to like me back.

Lush pastureland, a doting mom, and a red carpet are not enough to keep an equine happy. I knew if I didn't find Georgia a companion soon, her escapades into the larger world would continue. The dilemma, of course, was to find a horse friend for a horse hater, someone she wouldn't kill or maim or bully. It would be like trying to find a playmate for Leona Helmsley. Who could survive the moods, the tirades, the perpetual me-first-ness? I knew it would have to be a gelding, someone mature, big-hearted, and egoless. Someone who, no matter what, would never hold a grudge, a Nelson Mandela for my Leona. Anyone less could never handle the job.

Nelson Mandela may be one in a million among humans; however, among equines, Mandela's sterling attributes are much more common. It boils down to what horse lovers have always known: most horses are much nicer than most people. Not that this was evident in my pasture.

I didn't have to look for long. In fact, I didn't have to look at all. I don't remember how the subject of horses came up, but I found out that a woman named Donna who worked the cash register at the ski shop at Hunter Mountain was looking for a temporary place to keep her horse while she joined her husband on the West Coast for a six-month computer-training program.

Hotshot was a twenty-five-year-old chestnut-colored quarter horse who in his youth had been a barrel racer. I didn't know much about barrel racers except that besides bucking broncos, most rodeo horses are bulletproof; they seem unflapped by loud cheering crowds, bright fluttering colors, and unhappy charging bovines. Any horse who could doze through a rodeo seemed like a promising candidate to become Georgia's pasture mate.

Donna and I decided that the best way to introduce them would be to go for a ride together. Horses almost always behave better under saddle and on neutral turf. That way nobody has to "defend the castle" or "clarify" boundaries. Even Georgia recognized that beyond her fence, the rules of the universe changed somewhat. Out there, for instance, you could stamp your foot for a long time before someone might notice you needed an alfalfa treat *right now.*

Hotshot arrived on a sunny clear day in winter when there was hardly any snow on the ground. It was a good day for a trail ride with sure footing, and like all winter rides, it was blissfully free of bugs. Donna saddled Hotshot while he was still in the trailer, and I saddled Georgia in the turnout shed I'd built in the back pasture the previous summer. Before Georgia realized we had visitors, we all met for the first time in my neighbor's hay field. Henry didn't mind if I rode through his fields as long as I stayed on the edge, so it was a good place to meet in case Georgia needed space to work out any hostility, and Hotshot had plenty of room to escape.

It wasn't so bad. Georgia squealed several times but didn't strike, and Hotshot stood quietly, communicating clearly that he'd seen it all, and meeting a temperamental mare was nothing to get jazzed up about. They stood nose to nose for a few minutes, breathing each other in until both felt comfortable enough to notice they were standing on pretty good foraging material, and suddenly that became more interesting to them than waging war. After that, we rode together for a couple of hours on trails through the woods, with Georgia leading the way and never once displaying any ill feeling toward Hotshot. On the contrary, she seemed to enjoy his company because when occasionally he'd follow too close, her ears didn't flatten and her body language said that nothing about his presence threatened her. The most memorable thing about that ride was how unmemorable it was.

Back at the house, we took off their tack in the pasture with the turnout shed, and free of riders for the first time, the horses trotted across the field away from us and bent their heads to graze as though they'd been together for a long time. Hotshot was the same chestnut red as Georgia, and at first glance it was impossible to tell them apart.

It was clear from the beginning that we had found our Mandela. While Georgia seemed to like Hotshot — meaning she never seriously attacked him — there didn't seem to be a single thing Hotshot was allowed to do without Georgia's OK. When she gave the signal, they'd leave the turnout shed to graze. Later, during the summer, if it became too buggy or too hot or she'd had enough, she'd herd him back inside ahead of her. When she was thirsty, she'd drive him to the watering trough, and when I entered the pasture, Hotshot was forbidden to approach me. In fact, when I was around, Georgia could be at her most unreasonable. If I wanted to groom Hotshot or just spend time visiting him, the only way to do it was to preoccupy

Georgia with food. Otherwise she would rush at him with flattened ears to chase him off. Countless times during the day she would chastise him with a nip to the shoulder for crimes undetectable to the human eye. Hotshot never retaliated. He was sweet to the bone and a wonderful ride for any guest.

The last time I saw Donna was the day she dropped off her horse.

See you in six months, she said, waving to me as her truck pulled out of the driveway.

Is it possible that she left without giving an address or a phone number? Is it possible I would have allowed this? I must have, because a year later, when she still hadn't returned, I made an effort to find her, not because I wanted her to take her horse back but because I didn't. By then, Hotshot was mine, and it was impossible to imagine giving him up, even to the person who had been present at his birth and had owned him twenty-four years longer than I had.

It's amazing how easy it is to disappear. Short of hiring a private investigator, I made a concerted effort to find Donna, but every lead went cold. At first I was afraid I would never find her, but after a few years I was afraid I would. The best argument for why I got to keep Hotshot (if there was any argument at all) seemed to be desertion. And as the farrier and vet bills mounted, it seemed to me that at some point, I had a financial claim as well.

It took me a few years to understand why someone would abandon her horse. At first I believed it was a sign of gross indifference and irresponsibility, but in the end I came to the opposite conclusion. Donna had grown up learning to ride on Hotshot's mother, and when Hotshot was born, Donna had trained and competed on him in Western shows for more than fifteen years. That's a long time to spend with a horse every day. That's a lot of work and care and love. It must have been terrible for Donna to realize that her lifestyle could no longer sustain her horse. Maybe it was too painful to face. When she dropped him off at my farm that day, I don't think even she realized she was never coming back. The only way she could give up her horse at all was to tell herself it was only temporary. *I'll be back in six months,* she had said, and at the time she certainly seemed to believe it.

Still, for several years I jumped at the sound of any pickup truck pulling into my driveway and half expected to wake up one morning to find Hotshot gone. I mostly worried for Georgia, who, in her own way, had grown attached to Hotshot. When I'd take her out of the pasture in the early morning for our daily ride, she'd send out her most distressing calls to him and wouldn't stop until she could no longer hear his response, which meant the first half mile or so was more a Shakespearean tragedy than a fun ride. The possibility of Hotshot's departure worried me enough that when the opportunity to get another horse arose, I seized it.

I don't remember how I learned that someone named Judy was looking for a place to board her horse. I just remember standing at the end of my driveway on a windy fall day, watching a wild-eyed palomino ridden by a slender young woman prance down the road toward me, sideways. And so arrived Tempo, a sweet but anxious gelding, the same age as Hotshot, who stole Georgia's heart the second she met him. It was the first time she didn't squeal or strike at a new horse. When Judy led him into the pasture for the first time, Georgia followed him around like a puppy. Hotshot seemed equally enthralled, and thus, during those first moments together, Tempo was recognized as the herd's slightly neurotic but beneficent leader. Maybe it was his overly cautious nature — enough for all three of them — that made him leadership material. I don't know how horses decide these things, what suddenly says *presidential* about a certain horse to all the others, but it was clearly and immediately unanimous. Tempo was the man.

Unlike Donna, Judy remained a regular and important presence in our lives, coming to ride Tempo and to help me care for all three horses at least twice a week.

Although the turnout shed was fine for getting out of the rain and away from the bugs, it was no substitute for a barn. I'd never had to build a barn, so before I did, I visited as many barns as I could, noting important elements about each of them that I could incorporate into the design of mine — for example, leaving holes in the floor of the hayloft above each stall, so hay could be dropped down instead of carried down; putting in a horse-proof grain storage bin; kick-proofing the stall walls with two by fours; and making one stall a possible infirmary with a door to an outside pen for anyone who needed to be restricted.

It took several months to build the twenty-by-forty-foot, six-stall barn with a gable roof. Tim came from New Jersey to help the crew of four men with their assorted dogs. There was laughter on the property, the sound of voices and hammering and sawing mingling in the air with the cry of swallows who moved in before the last of the roof rafters were up. One weekend I helped shingle the roof, standing on the platform with the four men, doing a complete somersault in midair and landing on my feet when the platform collapsed under our weight. Miraculously, nobody was hurt, and we laughed so hard we had to sit on the upturned buckets and bags of cement to catch our breath.

I loved the sound of the men's trucks arriving in the morning, the sound of their dogs barking a greeting at Bear, who would lumber down to lift his leg on every truck and wag his tail among the workers searching for a bite of an egg sandwich or a doughnut. I loved that every morning all four men would wander over to the fence where the horses were and give them carrots or a sip of coffee or a good neck scratch before heading to the barn site to begin work.

I loved it, too, when the last of them would get in his truck at the end of the day, leaving me alone in the silence with only Bear and the horses and the swallows. I'd sit on the back deck with Bear in the diminishing light, watching the horses graze in the back field and the swallows dive for bugs across the surface of the pond, luxuriating in the notion that for the first time in my life, I was exactly where I was supposed to be. I had gathered together my own family and built a home for us.

I am in the back seat of a blue station wagon with my cousin Christie, and we are on our way to Weston, Massachusetts, where I will live with my aunt and uncle and their three daughters. The only ones who come to pick me up are Christie, who is my age, eight, and her mother. Laura and Holly are too young and are home with a babysitter. I don't know why I won't be living in Rye, New York, or Aiken, South Carolina, with my grandmother anymore or why I won't be taking riding lessons with Mr. Newman. I will not be driven to school by Franz. I think the reason is that I am bad. My grades are bad, and Franz says I leave scuff marks on the floor. Mr. Newman was mad at me for screaming when my horse reared, and Grandmother says I am a poor workman, which can mean a lot of things but mostly means she wishes I were someone else. I wish I were someone else, too, someone like my cousin Christie, who is artistic and smart and has two parents and a home.

My new room is small, with a window that looks out at the back door, which is the door where Tarnish meows to go out or come in during the middle of the night. I always wake up and open the door, and it makes me feel like I'm doing something important, as if I have a job nobody else can do or will do. As if I'm needed. At breakfast my aunt will say, *Susie, did you let Tarnish out last night?* I will nod and feel I've earned the right to be there.

I am afraid of my uncle because he is absolutely and utterly dependable and would never do anything impulsive or stupid, which is a hard standard to follow. Next to my uncle I see how "wrong" I am. Not that at eight years of age I think I am supposed to be "done," but I sense how far off the path I already am, how lost in fear and shame. My uncle cannot possibly be who he is and also be fond of someone like me. He never says a word, but I sense his disapproval, his dismay at having this alien among his people. I cannot escape my differentness. I cannot escape the fact that I am the daughter of a man who would leave and never come back.

I don't bring up my father because when his name is mentioned, it is never a good thing. My aunt tells how awful it was growing up with him because he never did what he was told and always caused trouble. He knocked her out by mistake once, pushing her into a radiator, where she hit her head. Another time he embarrassed her at a dance by becoming drunk and smoking cigarettes. He was twelve. It is the first time I hear the word *potential*. *Your father had such potential,* she says. Later, after she looks at my first report card, she says to me, *You have so much potential.* She sighs.

I sort of understand what it means, but not really. Potential for what? For sewing and drawing like my cousins? I don't really want to do those things, but maybe I *should* want to. Maybe I want the wrong things, like living with my father and Lloyd and pointing to a house and being able to say, *That's mine.* I want to belong. Nothing else seems important.

I am cold in Weston. I start getting cold in October, and the feeling never goes away all winter. My aunt and uncle keep the heat turned low because it is better for you, they say, but I am always freezing. I look forward to school because I know it will be warm. Later I shiver through dinner and afterward go to my room and wrap myself in a blanket. There is no television, so at night we do our homework, read a book, or talk in each other's rooms. Christie plays the piano, so sometimes I listen to her practice. She has beautiful hands, and I like to watch them move over the keys. I can't believe how smart she is. She can do anything, but she never brags. She never tells me I am dumb.

Grandmother sometimes sends Christie and me two of the same dresses, which I like to wear at the same time but Christie doesn't. In the morning before school, I wait for her to walk down the hall past my bedroom door, which I open wide enough to peek at what she's wearing and then quickly put on the same dress after it's too late for her to change. This drives Christie crazy, but I am thrilled that everyone at school knows we are connected, that I belong to Christie.

It is spring and I am still cold. I am waiting for something to happen, for my life to begin, for the exile to be over, for my father to come. Besides letting the cat in and out at night, I am not needed here. I am not one of them. I know it in a thousand ways, and yet none of them is bad. I cannot point to anything and say, *See, this is terrible. This is unfair.* And yet, I know I don't belong here. It is a truth so deep it needs no words. I don't look like them, I don't sound like them, and I don't even think like them. I see clearly the almost invisible wall around them, the indefinable thing that makes them a family, like a snow globe, a perfectly contained world, separate from everything. All of it makes me ashamed because it means I am the wrong one, the one who is different. But no matter what I do, I cannot change that, not even by wearing the same dress as Christie to school.

At the same time I know that there is no place else to go. Grandmother has sent me away, but even if she hadn't, I know I don't belong with her either. I don't belong with Franz. The idea of not belonging somewhere terrifies me. If I let myself think about it, my heart starts to pound and I have to go someplace where I can be alone and rock myself, or I will go crazy. Sometimes I go to my room and rock myself in bed, but it is better to go to the basement and get on one of the wooden rocking horses Christie and I ride together. There, without Christie to see my shaky, sweaty hands, I can get on a horse and gallop away from the thing on my chest that will crush me if I don't move. I can gallop and gallop and gallop to that place that exists in the future where I will belong.

Hanging out with the barn crew for a few hours each day seemed like just the right thing to ease me back into the human race. Their presence was a reminder of how isolated I had become, how I yearned for the company of my own kind. For months I had thought that living alone with my dog and horses would be enough, even ideal. Except for worrying about the nagging issue of money, which was quickly running out, accelerated by the construction of the barn, I had imagined a life where I would hardly ever have to leave the farm. But when the construction crew arrived with their dogs and their laughter and the stories of their wives and children, I began to remember what was good about human beings. I began to remember I was one of them.

Buying the house in Olivebridge had given me my first sense of home, and building the barn for Georgia made it feel complete. This was the farm I'd endlessly imagined as a child, and Georgia was the equine soul mate with whom I'd dreamed of sharing it. It was the first real home in which I'd felt secure enough to stop drinking and to begin to live a life that was both more honest and more authentic. And though part of me felt comfortable withdrawing from the world forever, the new sober part knew that if I wanted to keep my home and my horse, it was time to leave home. It was time to find a job.

Georgia's first winter in Olivebridge, 1983.

The house in Lake Placid on one hundred acres that I bought with money from my grandmother.

Georgia on the farm in Lake Placid with the new sunroom behind her.

Clowning around on the day of my second marriage in the farm house in Lake Placid, 1979. From left to right: Peter, a friend from Boston, my brother, my cousin Laura, my brother's first wife, Janet (upside down), me, and my husband.

A family ride in Lake Placid. From left to right: me standing next to Georgia, my husband on Nikka, his son on Thunder, with our dogs Issac, Bear, and Birdie.

Georgia on the red carpet in her new garage "stall" in Olivebridge.

Me on a morning ride on Georgia in Olivebridge, 1985.

Georgia and her foal in Olivebridge, thirty minutes after the birth.

Me with my geese, Pam and Franny, in the pond in Olivebridge.

A good view of the garden at my grandmother's house in Aiken (where Willie the drunken gardener spent most of his day sleeping).

Grandmother Richards at the loom in her weaving studio at the house in Rye, New York.

My father taking a test drive in his Holman Moody ocean racer just after he bought it from a dealer in Miami, 1973.

My dog Pilgrim on the farm in Olivebridge.

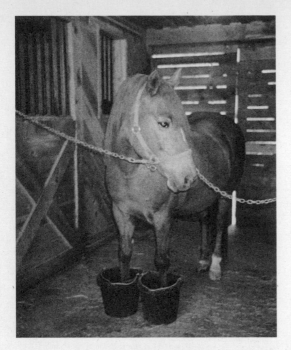

LEFT: *Georgia soaks in ice water during a bout with laminitis.*

BELOW: *Georgia clowning around in Lake Placid.*

{CHAPTER 6}

IT WAS SIX O'CLOCK on a spring morning, hours before the barn crew would arrive, and Henry's hay fields were shrouded in a heavy mist. Georgia trotted along the stone wall through the wet grass snorting her alarm as we passed a newly stacked pile of wood that hadn't been there the day before. I spoke to her softly and stroked her neck as I circled around to let her see the wood one more time. Stacks of logs always spooked her, so I made a point of stopping whenever we passed one. I didn't understand what frightened her about them, what in their shape or smell made her jump sideways at the sight. Sometimes I'd dismount, walk her right up to the pile, and urge her to give it a good sniff. She never would, and if I picked up a log to show her, she'd jerk herself backward and give me her wildest eye. This time I didn't press her, and after a second look, we trotted on, passed through the next opening in the stone wall, and entered the woods.

Stacked wood wasn't the only thing that frightened her. She was afraid of snakes, squirrels, bridges, and hummingbirds. If a squirrel ran across our path, she'd either stop dead in her tracks or buck. If she heard the buzz of a hummingbird, she'd bolt if I didn't hold her back. Every morning we crossed the same small concrete bridge, and every morning she'd stop before I urged her forward, and then she'd prance across it with her head held so high sometimes her forelock would flick across my face.

We'd seen a snake only once. It had slithered by before we'd even left the pasture, and she had reared and fled back to the turnout shed. Sometimes in the fall, blowing leaves would frighten her, and she always cocked her head and flared her nostrils at anything in my hand that looked "strange." I never knew what that might be. Once it was a paperback book, and another time it was a baby swallow that had fallen out of its nest.

Except for bridges, I never insisted she overcome her fears. Maybe because I didn't really think it was possible, but mostly because I didn't think it was necessary. She'd overcome them herself when she was ready. Who didn't have baseless fears? I was riddled with them and knew that no amount of reasoning would make them go away. I did for Georgia what I wished someone would do for me — patted her on the head and told her everything would be all right.

As I rode in the woods that spring morning, I was afraid

of the new job I'd be starting the next day. I was afraid of leaving the horses and meeting new people and doing things I'd never done before. I was afraid I'd fail.

I'd been worried about money, especially as I poured more and more of it into the barn, but I felt like such a wreck in my early sobriety I didn't know how I could possibly work. I wasn't certified to teach in New York, and I didn't want to go back to the ski business with the traveling, the drinking, and the ex-husband. Still, I knew I had to earn a living but had no idea how.

In the back of my mind, I'd always wanted to write, for as long as I could remember. One afternoon, with all the free time I had hiding from the world, I sat down and wrote a story about the time I came across a group of loggers in the woods while on a morning ride with Georgia. They had been debating what to do about a hawk's nest with two babies in an area they had planned to log that day. In the end they decided not to log there and climbed back in their trucks and drove away. Their kindness impressed me, so I wrote about it and sent it to a small weekly publication called *Lifestyle,* which featured human-interest stories from around the Hudson Valley. A few days later the editor called and offered thirty-five dollars for the piece.

Do you have anything else? he asked.

That simple question released a twenty-year logjam. Suddenly I found plenty to write about. I wrote a story about my neighbor Henry and another about my farrier, Bill Benson. I wrote about how bossy Georgia could be and how much Bear loved vanilla ice cream from Dairy Queen. I wrote about the people I bumped into around Olivebridge: the UPS driver who was afraid of my newly acquired pair of geese and the woman at the bookstore who trained guide dogs for the blind. *Lifestyle* took them all, and in exchange, every week, I received a small check.

Of course that was the trouble, the small check. It wasn't enough to live on. It wasn't even enough to keep Bear in ice cream. Then the editor called again. He was leaving his job. He asked whether I wanted to become the next editor of *Lifestyle*.

I hadn't interviewed for a job in a long time, and never for one I was so unequivocally unqualified to do. I couldn't spell. Without a dictionary stapled to my head, I was practically illiterate. I had to look up the spelling of words like *receive, occur,* and *success* or check words such as *every time* to see if they were one word or two. I was one of those teachers who, when writing something on the blackboard, would hear comments like, *Um, Miss Richards, isn't* class room *one word?*

The editor of anything should at the very least be a spelling and grammar genius and, in the case of a small publication, should know a lot about layout and design as well. I went for the interview anyway, because how could I not? I was almost broke. I had a bona fide anxiety attack through most of it but still landed the job. Either they were really desperate or I wasn't as dumb as I felt.

For days after I started this job, I was wracked with such anxiety about it that every morning as I drove to work, I rehearsed my quitting speech. The truth is, writing, the one requirement where I could claim any competence, was the least important part of the job. I was responsible for reading and editing submissions, taking photographs, designing and laying out the paper, writing a weekly column, and deciding what the overall theme should be for the next issue. The day before I started was the previous editor's last day of work, which meant there was no one there to train me, no one who could guide me through the step-by-step process of putting out a paper. For a job with a salary just above the federally defined poverty line, training was a luxury. The paper simply couldn't afford paying overlapping editors, not even for a week.

I trained myself by looking through back issues and talking to the staff in advertising and production. I even talked to the receptionist, an eighty-year-old woman named Hilda, who'd been there since the sixties and had seen a dozen editors come and go. She had no idea how to put together a paper, but she told me where to park my car. Sometimes I'd leave my desk to have a panic attack in the bathroom. When I told the publisher I was worried about the first issue, he smiled and said it would be just fine. No one but me seemed worried that a disaster might be in the making. Somehow I put that first paper together with a theme centered on swimming pools, and it looked OK.

Here's the first editorial I wrote in the spring of 1984, when I was thirty-four.

The standard format for any newly elected President of this country is to dispense with the inaugural address as quickly as possible and get on to the really important speech where he tells us about all the problems he's inherited from the previous administration, what we can't blame him for and why his hands are tied. By sufficiently lowering our expectations, now that we know how impotent and victimized he is, we're pleasantly surprised when he accomplishes anything. This seems like good PR to me and something everyone should do as soon as the new job is safely secured and the health insurance coverage activated.

As the new editor of *Lifestyle Magazine*, I have inherited some particularly nasty problems which, with the almost limitless power vested in me as editor, I will outline in this column (conveniently established by the previous administration).

The most bargain crazy shopper wouldn't pay a dollar for my chair at a garage sale. It hurts to sit on it, it hurts to look at it and it has to go. I've tried perching on the edge, sliding all the way back, adding a pillow and nothing works. Everyone else in the office has the same kind of chair and seems content. This makes me suspicious.

Every morning, along with fresh perked coffee, someone named Hilda, (or maybe it's Joan) brings in a sugary bombshell of a pastry, enough for everyone in the office to gorge on if they want to. Minutes after arriving at the office, I'm dripping gooey apple strudel on manuscripts marked "please return" and I just want you to know who to blame (Hilda or Joan) and why the paper might look smudgy.

When a *Lifestyle* issue is put together and ready to go, it gets sent to our corporate headquarters to be printed. Does anyone know where this is or how to pronounce it? Cana-ja-hairy? I can't even fake it phonetically and wish someone would say it slowly, just once, so I could find it on a map. I don't think it's nice of them to make me look so stupid. They could have picked Albany. Everyone can at least pronounce it.

In spite of these problems, I was able to get out my first issue of *Lifestyle*. Now that you're familiar with them, (the problems) I think you'll agree it was a considerable accomplishment. Just think what I could do with a good chair, clean copy and a map.

Even worse than finding myself doing a job I wasn't qualified to do was the fact that it took me away from the horses and Bear. For the first time since owning them, I had a nine-to-five job, which several days a week became nine to nine. It felt like I was never home, as though I had completely abandoned them. Fortunately, Bear was the kind of dog who would never abandon the property, so I could leave him in the house to come and go as he pleased through a dog door. He could walk himself down to the pond for a frog hunt and a swim, or he could keep the horses company by lying on the cool concrete floor of the center aisle of the barn. Still, we had spent twenty-four hours a day together since he was a puppy. It must have been lonely for him to suddenly find me gone.

The horses were another matter. When I first started the job, at least twice a week I'd come home to find them standing at the end of the driveway, apparently waiting for my car. There was no telling how long they'd been out, but just the fact that they were in the driveway and not grazing suggested they had gorged to capacity on the too-rich lawn. Where else might they have been? Strolling on the road through traffic? OK, Olivebridge didn't really have traffic, but all it takes is one car to do the unthinkable to a horse. The point is, I wasn't there to know. I wasn't there to ride or feed or groom or stare at them over the fence because just being in their presence was enough to make me feel that I was doing something fabulous. I missed them. I felt robbed of the best part of my life.

Eventually they became used to my schedule and stopped knocking the fence down looking for me. I also started getting up earlier in order to have more time with them. Instead of riding at six, I'd ride at five and sometimes even earlier. I often rode when it was still dark, watching the sun rise across my neighbor's hay fields as I headed back to the barn after an hour's ride in the woods with Bear in tow.

It was Georgia who helped me through the early days at *Lifestyle.* It was the peace of those morning rides full of the smells of a dew-drenched earth and my own precious horse. It was the unburdening of all my fears to the pair of large ears that flickered attentively at the sound of my voice, no doubt picking up the tone of despair they heard, if not quite the facts. It was the hour I spent in the barn, my church, the hour of silent thanks for all the ways my life was good, including the new job, which even from the beginning held at least the possibility of new friendships.

However, it was Georgia who defined me, who provided the centerpiece of my life and around whom everything else was built. I had left a bad marriage in order to give her safety, had built her a home, and had filled it with siblings. For her, I had stopped drinking, recognizing that sobriety was as essential to parenting a horse as it was to parenting a child. For her, I wanted to be better, to be worthy, to be whole. For her, I wanted to be human.

The intensity of the love I felt for my animal family and for Georgia in particular was not something I spoke about often. I suppose I was afraid of being labeled eccentric or antihuman, neither of which was true. I simply felt that animal children were the equal of human children and deserved the best of whatever I had to give. And leaving them alone for most of the day to go to a full-time job was a blow to the kind of life I had hoped to provide for them.

It didn't take long to convince the publisher that my layout and design talents really were nil, so he let me hire an assistant with strong graphic skills. Thus, into our lives came the wonderful and talented Lane Ackerman, who made the paper gorgeous and kept us laughing harder than anyone could remember. Lane became the most beloved person on our staff and the first real friend I made since moving to the area. The women were in love with him, and the men wanted to be him; at least they wanted whatever it was that made him so magnetic to women, young and old alike. I felt the kind of love for Lane that I felt for my brother, the brother who was a virtual stranger after we were separated but had become closer to my heart than I could easily put into words. Lane and I fought like siblings, too. I'd arrive at work in the morning, probably obnoxiously perky, flashing a kind of in-your-face sobriety (I mean, who *else* wakes up to ride at 4:30 A.M. except some crazy ex-drunk), to find Lane half asleep and hung over from yet another all-night bender.

Did you shoot those photos we need for today? I'd ask at 9:01 A.M., leaning across the top of my spotless desk.

Just give me a few minutes here, he'd answer, barely able to raise his head above the mess of his desk.

Because we need to figure out ad space.

Just a sip or two of coffee, okay?

You did shoot them, right?

It's nine o'clock, for Christ's sake.

Nine o'five.

Fuck you.

No, fuck you.

By lunch we'd be on level ground, me with less perk and Lane with more caffeine, and work on the paper would be humming along. By late afternoon I'd be punch-tired, but that's when Lane came to life. I wish I could remember some of the funny things he said, the way he'd get the whole office laughing until we hurt. But I just remember the effects, how the typesetters would suddenly stand up, laughing so hard they had to cross their legs to keep from peeing. How the publisher, ordinarily a reticent figure who didn't mingle much with the rest of us, would lean against the wall with his hands in his pockets, jiggling change, trying to look dignified through uncontrollable laughter.

Much of Lane's humor was self-deprecating. In spite of his many talents as a writer, photographer, graphic designer, cartoonist, guitar maker, musician, and builder (he helped finish building my barn, adding a gargoyle-like galloping wooden horse he had carved at the peak of the roof and a spiral staircase to the hayloft), he suffered from enormous self-doubt and believed he was a failure. One of his funniest and most revealing cartoon series was about a character he called the Country Guy. It featured a slightly disheveled man wearing a suit and carrying a briefcase, on his way to New York City to try to find a publisher for his novel. In each frame, from the man boarding the train to walking through the streets of Manhattan to looking dejected in front of the desk of some disapproving editor, there are chicken feathers falling out of his briefcase or the pockets of his suit or the back of his collar. In some of the frames, the character has brought a whole chicken with him, as in the one where a chicken foot is sticking out of the shut briefcase and in another when he's carrying a chicken tucked under his arm. It was how Lane saw himself—a silly country boy with impossible literary dreams.

Never had I met anyone so gifted in so many ways who was so unable to see it. I don't think there was a single person who met Lane who didn't eventually feel the need to save him, to rescue him from his terrible and inaccurate self-image. It must have been part of his appeal to women and perhaps to men as well. He was someone everyone wanted to protect, but in the end no one could.

Years after we had both left the paper, Lane's adored young son died in a house fire. The tragedy proved too much for this sensitive and gentle father, and not long afterward, Lane, still a young man, was found dead in his own bed. No doubt alcohol was involved. Lane had struggled with it for years, but I think he really died from a broken heart. And what an enormous heart it had been.

One morning in April, as I ran a quick brush across the underside of Georgia's belly, I felt a hard mass. I was so shocked, I recoiled from her and was unable to recheck it. Instead, I stared at her for a moment; she seemed content as she ate her grain, and I looked her over from head to tail for some sign of the terrible illness I immediately assumed she had. Nothing that hard could be anything but cancer. My horse might have looked fine, but the mass could only mean she was dying. I took a deep breath and checked her one more time, extending a trembling hand under her belly, feeling along until I bumped into it again. *Oh, God.* She wasn't even six years old yet.

I dropped the brush and ran back to the house on shaky

legs to call the vet. I explained what I had felt and where it was, all the way back tucked up high in her abdomen; her teats, in fact. *They're hard as rocks,* I cried. *Please come!*

I couldn't bear to go back to Georgia while I waited for the vet. I couldn't bear to face my dying horse. I didn't leave the house until an hour later, when I heard the vet's truck pull down my driveway and park near the back pasture where Georgia stood in the turnout shed. He was a good man, a vet who had never done anything more complicated with my three horses than vaccinate and worm them. This was our first medical crisis, our first life-and-death nightmare. I was so rattled I could hardly speak to him. I was afraid if I opened my mouth, I'd lose control and be unable to assist in whatever he might need me to do. Draw blood? Take a biopsy? Euthanize her on the spot?

Well, let's just see what we have here, he said peering under her belly as I held her still with one hand on her halter, stroking her beautiful face with the other. I could tell Georgia didn't like him by the wildness in her eye and because she danced away from him on the lead line, making it difficult for him to examine her. Her distrust of the vet embarrassed me because he was gentle and kind, and there was no reason for her animosity. I felt like the mother of a child who when the child meets her teacher for the first time declares, *I hate you!*

I'm sorry, I said, unable to keep her from moving away from him. The more he tried to touch her, the more agitated Georgia became, until she was rearing up at him as soon as he approached.

We'll have to twitch her, he said, walking back to the truck to get the twitch.

As soon as he had her lower lip twisted in it, she froze in place, terrified but quiet. Twitching is so uncomfortable that even the wildest horse will stand quietly to avoid giving herself more pain. After his first good look under her belly, he walked back to the truck and returned with two long latex gloves.

You put one on, too, he said, throwing one of the gloves to me and putting the other one on himself. It covered his arm all the way to his shoulder. *I think I know what's going on, but I'm going to give her a pelvic exam just to be sure.* His voice sounded incredibly cheerful for someone examining a horse who was about to die.

After lubricating his arm well, he lifted Georgia's tail and slowly inserted his hand into her birth canal. *Yup,* he said in a few minutes. *There's definitely a good-size foal in there. I'd say she only has another week or two to go.*

No wonder Georgia hated him. He was a complete idiot. *She's never been bred,* I said, embarrassed for him that he was so far off the mark on this one. Had he even finished vet school?

Well, he chuckled, turning the glove inside out as he pulled it down, snapping it off his hand at the end. *Let me hold the twitch, and you get yourself at the other end for a look-see. Be sure to use plenty of lubricant. Go ahead,* he urged when I hesitated. *See what you can find down there.*

I'd never stuck my hand in Georgia's mouth, let alone into the deepest cavity of her body. I felt more than squeamish about it, but between my horror at her illness and my deep skepticism of the vet's qualifications to practice medicine, I wasn't in my right mind and did what I was told. I put on the glove, lubricated my arm, and started easing my hand downward just under her tail. I followed the contours of her body until I came to what felt like a big open space, and that was where I bumped into something rock hard, which I traced with my fingers. A tiny hoof! I kept feeling around, and right near the hoof I bumped into something else hard. Teeth!

Oh, my God! I said over and over again. *How did this happen?*

Two weeks later Georgia gave birth to a healthy bay filly who must have been conceived during the time my husband had hidden Georgia on the farm in Vermont. I tried hard to be present for the birth by spending nights sleeping in the loft of the turnout shed, but Georgia had her baby during the twenty minutes it took me to walk back to the house and take a shower one morning. When I returned, there was the foal, already nursing as mother and foal stood in the middle of the pasture in a chilly rain.

From the beginning, Georgia was a relaxed mother, allowing me and any other human who wanted to visit her baby plenty of latitude to do it. On that first morning, as the two stood in the rain, Georgia let me walk right up to her and take her gently by the halter to lead her and her baby out of the rain and into the turnout shed I had prepared especially for the occasion with a deep layer of cedar chips. Tempo and Hotshot were at a safe distance in the other pasture across the pond, within sight but not close enough to make Georgia feel the least bit anxious about their grazing too near her foal. It was a thrilling morning to welcome this unexpected and healthy filly into our lives. I felt as close to being a grandmother as I ever imagined I could feel. The foal was sweet and trusting and let me handle her right from the start. I named her Sweet Revenge because she was something wonderful that had come from something terrible: my separation from her mother and the ugly divorce. Now this happy ending, this bit of harmless revenge! I called her Jenny and sent out birth notices to everyone I could think of.

A few weeks after Jenny was born, I jumped on Georgia bareback and rode her around the pasture to see what her foal would do. At first she frisked along beside us, circling her mother at a trot, flattening her ears at me as she bolted past, brushing my leg with her side. Then she started bucking and rearing, her skinny front legs pawing at the air, sometimes coming within inches of hitting me. Every time she did this, I'd give her a stern *No!* and turn Georgia's hindquarters toward her. Eventually she stopped and trotted beside her mother, looking elegant on long slender legs that were clumsy when she tried to stand up or lie down. Every day for a week, I rode Georgia bareback around the back pasture until Jenny trotted or cantered beside us without pinning her ears at me and without bucking or kicking.

At the end of the week, I opened the pasture gate and rode Georgia up the path and through the rock wall to Henry's fields. Jenny ran beside us, ears straight up and tail cocked with fear and excitement at all the new sights. She stayed close to her mother's shoulder, snorting her feelings as she frisked across Henry's hay field and into the woods on the other side. I didn't go far, less than half a mile up the path, just far enough to introduce the foal to the terrain crowded with trees and filled with so many new smells. Over and over, Jenny lifted her head to snort her alarm into the air. It was hard to tell if she was full of fear or full of bravado, but Georgia remained a steady, calm presence next to her baby. As we came back down the path that led to our own pasture, just before turning into the gate, Jenny stopped dead in her tracks and, lifting her head, sent a high-pitched whinny to Hotshot and Tempo, who were standing pressed against the gate in the pasture across the pond. They both answered her, and I like to think that was the beginning of what would eventually become a warm friendship between Jenny and her two doting "uncles."

A month later, at 5 A.M., a fuzzy pink light was just beginning to backlight the trees on the edge of Henry's hay field. Bear panted at Georgia's heel, ready for a cooling swim in the pond after the hour-long trek through the humid dawn of a warm June morning. Jenny trotted at Georgia's shoulder, circling back to occasionally "snowplow" Bear with her nose, her step quick and light, eager to return to nurse and to eat her morning grain.

Before me lay my entire farm with the almost perfectly round pond surrounded by yellowing hay fields divided by stone walls. To the right of the pond was a small glass house with a yellow striped awning fluttering over the back deck, and in the foreground, the newly built barn, crowned with its galloping-horse gargoyle. Tempo and Hotshot stood pressed against the fence with arched necks and intent eyes, waiting for the first glimpse of Georgia and Jenny as they crested the hill of Henry's field.

In a couple of hours I would be on my way to work as the editor of *Lifestyle Magazine,* a most humble publication but one that during the first year had given me the biggest personal and professional challenge I'd had to face in my new, fragile sobriety. I'd faced some terrible fears, and along with my newfound confidence, I'd made my first friends there, connecting me to my new community in a way I'd never felt connected anywhere before.

But my worse fear had been that a job would separate me from Georgia, how working from nine to five would change our relationship and make us more distant. I never wanted to be one of those owners who saw their horses only on weekends and spent all their time trying to undo the behavior problems caused by neglect. We had enough to deal with trying to overcome Georgia's fear of bridges, log piles, hummingbirds, and the rest. I didn't want to add new issues. Instead, our morning rides kept our bond strong, and now we had the fun of raising a foal together.

I suppose if any shadow was lingering in my life that day, it was one that had been there for as long as I could remember. I had yet to define it clearly, but I would have described it as a kind of fathomless sadness, complicated by guilt—how could I feel sad when I had so much? There it all was, stretched out before me: the writing job, the house, the horses, the end of alcoholism.

I wouldn't get to the bottom of that sadness for years to come, but that day I hugged Georgia and Jenny hard, and later, in a room full of laughter and camaraderie, I sat on an uncomfortable wooden chair to write a smokin' good story.

{CHAPTER 7}

A YEAR AFTER I stopped drinking, a friend visiting me from Boston dragged me to an AA meeting.

I have a horse, I said with unbridled (no pun intended) contempt as she pulled into the parking lot of a church. *I'm the editor of a newspaper,* I threw in, trying to impress her with my OK-ness. I'd been sober for a year, and I thought things were going pretty well. But the truth is I thought mostly men with bloodshot eyes and distended livers went to AA, that the two of us would walk into a smoke-filled room full of a bunch of babbling wet brains. I was horrified as I followed her into the church basement that first meeting, horrified that I was about to so publicly brand myself a drunk. It was one thing if I knew, but why did everyone else have to know?

What if someone sees us? I whispered.

Oh, shut up, she said, shoving me ahead of her toward the smell of coffee.

It wasn't my first AA meeting. I'd been to one once before with this same friend when we had decided to quit drinking together a year earlier. The difference was that she had continued going to meetings and I hadn't. I don't remember what I had thought of that first meeting, prob-ably because I'd still been drunk from the night before. It's possible I was in a blackout, something that had begun to happen more and more toward the end of my drinking phase.

I was so resistant to attending that second meeting, nothing prepared me for the profound sense of belonging I felt as soon as I began listening to the other alcoholics speak. Never had I identified so quickly and completely with a group of people. Not even with horse lovers had I felt such an affinity. Here was a tribe who really spoke my language: lonely, isolated, fearful, and insecure no matter what their lives looked like on the outside. Never could I have imagined such candor, such a willingness to discuss honest thoughts and feelings.

It was the first time I understood what being sober meant. Until I entered that room, I thought being sober meant not drinking. I didn't know it meant taking a per-sonal inventory — identifying your character flaws, all the ways in which you were responsible for your own failings, including anxiety or self-centered fear, as AA called it. It was the first time I considered that anxiety might be rooted in a kind of inflated self-importance, that even being shy had a component of false deference. Who were you to declare yourself so unavailable or so perfect that not living up to your own measure should make you withdraw? Should make you drink?

I didn't know that becoming sober meant *really* changing. Not drinking was the least of it. It was the rest of me that was the problem, the part that wanted to stay numb. The men and women in that room didn't sound numb anymore. They were angry and scared and depressed. They were also hopeful and funny and grateful. They were all over the place. The word that came to mind was *whole*. After years of shutting down all or parts of themselves with alcohol, they were finally whole human beings.

I sat in a corner with my arms crossed and my mouth shut and listened to what whole human beings sounded like. Evidently being human was a messy business. Not a single person said *Everything's fine* — my stock response since I was a child to any question about my state of mind. It had never been true, but that didn't keep me from repeating it for the next twenty years. I thought that's what you were supposed to say. I thought that's what you were supposed to *feel*. Anything else meant you were a complainer or worse — a bad person, a wrong person, and *wrong* was just a code word for crazy. I didn't want to be bad or crazy because I was already on shaky ground in the wantable department. So the sweet smiley girl became the sweet smiley woman who drank liquor to help keep the lid on anything that didn't reflect how fine she felt one hundred percent of the time. Never mind the on-and-off suicide fantasies going back to fourth grade. Doesn't everybody have those? I was fine.

When my friend left to go back to Boston, she made me

promise I'd keep going to AA. I would have gone anyway. Even though it made me uncomfortable and I hardly said a word, I liked that it was a place where people spoke the truth. After years of lying to myself about everything, hearing the truth was both horrible and fascinating. I wanted to hear more. I couldn't believe there was a place where people openly admitted the extent of their foibles, and that's putting it nicely. AA was full of disaster stories, with people both the victims and the perpetrators of their own destruction, and I was no exception. I'd driven drunk too many times to count and hoped only that I wouldn't get caught, never once considering the lives of everyone else on the road. When I finally wrecked the car one night driving home from a bar in Lake Placid, I blamed it on the snow, even though I'd been so drunk I didn't remember the accident until I saw the car the next morning, the driver's side bent in a U-shape where it had wrapped itself around a guard rail.

Like so many other decisions in my life, my marriage had been a product of alcoholic thinking. My husband liked to drink as much as I did, which meant I could fudge everything else, such as the fact that I hardly knew him, that we had little in common, or that he was a schmuck. I was no prize either, which meant he was lying to himself, too. In retrospect, we found exactly what we had asked for; we were two people willing to pretend they were somebody they were not. It mattered only that we looked good—the handsome guy and the pretty horse and the sweet farm in Lake Placid I could describe in letters to family and friends at a distance. I was desperate for somebody to believe the illusion because if they did, it would be true and I could ignore that nagging little voice that kept saying, *Huh?*

Besides my marriage, the scariest thing that ever happened to me was attending a sales meeting while in a blackout. My husband was in Europe, so I had to fly alone to the meeting in Aspen for one of the product lines we were representing in our ski business. The meeting lasted four days, but I don't remember any of it. The only way I knew I'd been there were the snippets of information I heard later about what I'd done or said from others who had been there and the copious notes I had taken every day during the meetings. The amazing thing was nobody knew I was in a blackout; nobody realized I was that drunk. It was one of those conferences with mimosas for breakfast, beer with lunch, and cocktails all night. Everyone must have been buzzed, but I was far beyond that. The couple in whose house I had been a guest told me that one night I brought back a man I'd met at a bar. They were giggling as they reminisced, as though openly committing adultery during a sales meeting with other professionals from all over the world was the best idea ever.

I remember that when I returned to Lake Placid, I was only mildly disturbed that I couldn't recall the previous four days. I had the notes to prove I was there, a slight sunburn from the afternoon we had all gone skiing, and a whole new sample line of ski clothing. What else mattered? I pushed the amnesia out of my mind along with all the other evidence of a serious alcohol problem and went out for dinner and drinks with friends.

Alcohol was at the root of many heartbreaking stories in AA, a tightly wound spiral of cause and effect that sometimes went back for generations. Nobody came out looking pretty, but nobody at AA thought trying to look pretty mattered anymore. It was the perfect place for someone who believed life was supposed to be lived between a stiff upper lip and a smiling one, and anything else needed to be tidied up fast with the help of a drink. I was hooked. It would be a long time before I participated much, but I watched and listened, already transformed by the novelty of hearing the truth.

In 1986, when Georgia was eight years old and I'd been sober for three years, she had her first bout with laminitis, which is also called founder. She was crosstied in the center aisle of the newly finished barn and stood in two buckets of ice water. Laminitis is a painful swelling of the tissue beneath the hoof, painful because the swelling has nowhere to go and pushes against the hard hoof wall. Sometimes it was a challenge to keep her from lifting her front feet out of the buckets and tipping them over, sending me back to the house for more ice so we could start all over again. This time I distracted her with a mound of hay and a good brushing. Tempo, Hotshot, and Jenny stood nearby, unwilling to leave the barn without her.

When the thirty-minute soak was done, I lifted a heavy hoof across my bent knee, dried it with a towel, applied hoof ointment, and wrapped it in layers of cotton gauze and over that layers of duct tape to keep the dressing attached to her hoof. In the unlikely event she didn't yank her hoof away and put it down on the dirty floor, which would have meant starting all over again, I squeezed the now-enormous hoof into a blue rubber "sneaker" to provide additional padding. My working on one foot required that she put all her front weight on the other foot, which was still soaking. It was a lot to ask of her, and sometimes she was in too much pain to do it, which meant if she didn't yank the foot away, she would transfer more and more of her weight to the hoof in my lap and gradually I'd be supporting about five hundred pounds. This was hard on my already bad back and exhausted us both. Still, the feet had to be soaked twice a day during the acute phase, which could last a week or more, and once a day after that until she improved.

Because of her illness, I spent more time with her out of the saddle. With both of us on the ground, she was more herself, more expressive. After all, on the ground we were eye to eye, a shift in the power dynamics that did not escape her. Georgia's body language had a roughness that sometimes bordered on aggression. Before she became sick, in the morning as I walked across the pasture toward the barn, she'd run in circles around me, bucking and kicking, nipping at Hotshot and Tempo and Jenny, all of it playful, but there was more horse poundage flying through the air near me than I wanted. If there was snow on the ground, she was worse, galloping her joy around the whole pasture, ending with a dead run straight at me. At the last possible second, she'd skid herself to a stop in front of my angry voice. Before she could take off again, I'd grab her halter and make her walk next to me the rest of the way to the barn, forcing her to stand still anytime she so much as put a spring into her step.

After she had laminitis, that changed. A serious illness can be humbling, and it humbled Georgia. She once had no reason to believe that her body could fail or that humans, me in particular, could be helpful. Although she was bored while soaking in ice, she learned it brought her some relief from pain and grew to tolerate it. I'd give her an oral dose of a nasty-tasting painkiller, which she also gradually came to accept without a battle because, no doubt, she was able to connect it to the relief that followed. I had three tons of fine-grade sand trucked in to cover the floor of her stall, as well as the ground of the small outside paddock attached to her stall. Its more forgiving surface provided additional cushioning for the painful hooves and enabled her to join the herd outside in the sun, albeit confined to her paddock.

She began to connect all of these pain-relieving measures to me, and it earned me both her gratitude and her affection. After she recovered from laminitis, she never ran at me again and, in general, pushed and shoved at me less aggressively. We bonded, the only good thing to come out of her ordeal.

During her illness, instead of riding for an hour before leaving for the paper, I spent an hour in the barn nursing Georgia, brushing out tails and manes, and doing barn projects. I never ran out of projects, partly because horses are so destructive (I repaired fences at least once a week) and partly because I enjoyed any excuse to spend time in the barn or pasture. And wherever I was, the horses were never more than a few feet away. They'd stand so close, I had to push them away if I was swinging a hammer. Tools lying on the ground next to me were picked up and nibbled. The wooden handles on hammers, shovels, and wheelbarrows had teeth marks.

Their favorite "tool" was the car. I'd built the barn in the middle of the pasture, so I had to drive the car across it to unload fifty-pound bags of grain, wood chips, and other supplies. While I unloaded, the horses would stand around the car licking it, nibbling side-view mirrors and windshield wipers; once, Georgia bit off the antenna. My car was always smeared with horse spit, and the interior smelled of manure.

One morning, as I struggled to wrap Georgia's hoof, the weight on my knee seemed minor compared to the weight on my mind. At age thirty-six, I was back to the same horrible problem, back to where I'd found myself too many times before — involved with the wrong man. Why did I keep picking liars? This time it was Tim, the man who had helped me move from Lake Placid to Woodstock and then Olivebridge. He'd driven the moving van, rounded up his friends to help with heavy furniture, and later had helped build the barn. He lived and worked in New Jersey, but for almost four years, he had made the two-hour drive north to spend weekends with me in Olivebridge. It was an arrangement that had suited us both, an exclusive relationship, but with plenty of elbowroom. It seemed ideal for two people who had no intention of marrying.

Tim traveled a lot for his marketing job at a private jet company. Sometimes several weekends would pass before he'd come north. I was used to these separations and thought nothing of them. Depending on the season, we'd spend the weekends riding, skiing, or hiking, sharing our love for the outdoors. I knew most of his friends in New Jersey, and he knew the handful of mine in Olivebridge.

Once, for a few months, we thought we should take steps to get closer, but when we didn't do anything about it (neither of us was willing to move), we agreed to see a therapist to help us clarify our feelings. The only thing I remember from the handful of sessions we attended was both of us being asked to describe what we saw in an inkblot. Tim saw a couple embracing, and I saw two fighting cats, skinned and bleeding to death. Clearly I was the crazy

one, seeing death where there was love. What else could
we conclude?

Months later, I answered the phone on a late Friday afternoon. A woman identified herself as Monica and told
me that she was in love with Tim. For more than an hour
I listened to astounding things, the most astounding of
which was that she and Tim had been living together in
New York City for the previous three years. They had
skied together in Colorado, had attended polo matches in
Greenwich, and had a joint membership at the New York
City Athletic Club. She told me that for three years she had
selected all my birthday and Christmas presents. She knew
what kind of books I liked, what size I wore, and where
I liked to eat. She cried through most of the phone call,
and at the end she said, *Do you still want him? Because if you
don't, I do.*

She didn't tell me why it had taken her three years to ask
me this question or why suddenly she had decided to ask
it now. Before I could answer her, and before I could ask
her why she would want such a person — because that's
what I really wanted to know — I heard Tim's car pull into
the driveway and we had to hang up. I had been sitting at
the kitchen counter, but when I stood up, my knees were
wobbly, and I had to steady myself before I could move. I
opened the door but kept the screen locked while I waited
for Tim to walk up the front steps. When he did, I stared
at him through the screen and asked, *Who are you?*

He laughed, thinking I was making a joke, but then I
said, *I just got off the phone with someone named Monica.*

At that point, nothing he said should have surprised me,
but his answer was so perfect in the last-thing-on-earth-
you'd-expect category, that even after an hour of mind-

blowing revelations, he was able to shock me one more time.

Does this mean you're going to have an attitude all weekend?

It wasn't particularly satisfying to slam the door in his face. It felt like such a small gesture compared to the enormity of the betrayal. I sometimes wondered what would have happened if I'd had a gun in my hand.

For weeks afterward, I went to work in a fog and spent nights staring at the ceiling wondering what was going to become of me. I lost fifteen pounds. I put the house up for sale. I couldn't imagine living there anymore, defiled as it was by the memory of having had such a man in it. When my realtor asked where I was moving, I said I didn't know. When she asked why I was moving, I said I didn't know that either. *Do you have anyone you can talk to?* she said, backing out the door.

I talked to Georgia in the mornings and evenings as I soaked her front feet and later when she was better, as we went for short rides around Henry's fields. I had stopped drinking so I could become someone responsible enough to take care of a horse, someone responsible enough to trust. Yet, I'd brought another monster into our lives. I'd screwed up stone-cold sober. *I don't know what to do,* I told Georgia. *I don't know where to go.* Nowhere and nothing felt safe. Someone had lied to me every single day for three years, and I'd never seen it, never felt it. *What's wrong with me?* I'd asked Georgia. It was a new kind of lost. I was missing a reflex as simple as blinking, as ordinary as pulling my hand from the heat. Instead, I was running *into* the burning building. No matter where I went, I kept finding Tims. Over and over.

Then I remembered the bloody fighting cats from the

Rorschach tests and knew I'd known. Somewhere deep and hidden, even from myself, was someone who knew the score. But how could I wake her up? How did she become the one in charge? I lay in bed every night that winter and wondered where I'd go and what I'd do. I never wanted to trust another human being.

As isolated and scared as I had felt during my first few months of not drinking—when a dead author, a dog, and a horse seemed to be the only company I could handle—the winter I asked Tim to leave was worse. I did my job at the paper and then went home, afraid that if I socialized with coworkers, they'd eventually ask where Tim was, and I was too ashamed to tell them what had happened. I blamed myself for his behavior in the sense that I was afraid there was some vibe I put out, something akin to a *kick me* sign, only mine was on my face or in my eyes   somewhere everyone but me could see, making me an easy target.

The truth is that although I looked independent—I owned my home, worked as the editor of a paper, took care of my animals, and paid my bills—it was only because Tim had been there, however infrequently, that I had been able to maintain that front. Without him to anchor me, to make me feel like someone had my back, the charade of my independence fell apart. I was terrified of being alone, not in the sense of spending time by myself but in the sense of not having someone central in my life, someone to take charge. I'd had one boyfriend or another since I was fifteen, with almost no alone time in between. For over twenty years I'd either been in a relationship or just begun or ended one. I didn't even think of myself as Susan. I was Tim's girlfriend or Peter's or Don's because if I didn't belong to somebody, I was nobody.

As I lay in bed that winter full of night terrors, I began to realize that those were old feelings, feelings that went much further back than the first boyfriend, all the way to my first memories — memories of being left, of not belonging to anyone. At five years old I couldn't have understood death, but I understood it enough to know that when our mother died, it meant Daddy was more important than ever — that our lives belonged to him after that. And I understood, too, that when he left, it was different from the way our mother had left. I understood that he was still there, somewhere I couldn't see or visit, but that he was coming back, and all I had to do was listen for the sound of his car in the driveway, and when I heard it, I would belong to someone again.

I knew how to wait. I knew how to survive living with my grandmother and later with my aunt and uncle and later still with my grandfather and Jean. I knew how to survive holidays visiting a variety of cousins and going to camp and boarding schools and summer schools or Europe and all the places my grandmother arranged for me to go because I had no home. I had gone to all those places and never once, not even in Europe, had I stopped waiting for the sound of his car to pull into the driveway. Never once had the wish to belong to him again diminished in the least. I had waited for my father until I was eighteen, the age Grandmother's legal guardianship of me would expire, and after that, if my father still didn't show up, I would officially belong to nobody.

Not surprisingly, my father didn't come. And not so surprisingly, when I was nineteen, I married Peter, a man with the same name as my father, a kind, loving man who brought a mother and a father and siblings into the bargain, and finally I belonged to something as solid as the television family the Waltons, and stopped waiting for the sound of my father's car in the driveway. I was too old to be Peter's daughter, so instead I became another Peter's wife. There wasn't much difference; it was still mostly a transfer of feeling from one man to another.

I was married in an old pink dress I had originally bought at Bonwit Teller for an eleventh-grade dance. I don't know why I decided pink was right. Maybe because it was the only dressy dress I had, and Peter and I were saving our money so we could drive out west, find an apartment, and go to school.

But I had been terrified to marry. Neil Armstrong had recently landed on the moon, but marrying seemed harder and scarier, too. All through the wedding at Peter's sister's house, I carried a frozen smile while we exchanged vows and then ate a roast turkey dinner with wedding cake afterward. Four nieces and nephews ran around the house playing, and Peter's ninety-five-year-old grandfather with half-inch-thick glasses sat in the chair by the window looking stern. Everyone else smiled and talked as if it was a normal day except for the briefest of interruptions to say *I do* and exchange a couple of borrowed rings because we didn't have enough money to buy our own. But who needed rings? We'd signed a scary-looking paper with a seal that said we were legally bound, but no matter how much that freaked me out, the state of Massachusetts and the United States government didn't care. I was Susan Swartz now. It was done.

In changing my name, I hadn't just severed myself from one family so I could belong to another, I'd severed myself from myself. Who knew it would feel so huge? It was as if

I had pulled out a mask and a costume that I would now wear forever: the Susan Swartz costume. I had no idea who she was, but she went through the day smiling — the same way the other Susan always had. But with that new costume, she'd gone even farther than Neil Armstrong. She was really out there — way, way, way past the moon.

Seventeen years later, agonizing over feeling abandoned again, I understood for the first time that I'd had no choice when I'd married Peter. He had given me the kind of security I needed to function. I was too fearful, too full of anxieties to make it alone. I was too needy. When the marriage ended a year and ten months later, not even a week went by before there was someone else, and from then until Tim, there had always been someone. There had always been a man's car to listen for in the driveway. I was as needy as ever.

The morning after I slammed the door on Tim, I dragged myself out of bed and went to the barn. If I hadn't had horses to get me up, I don't know if I would have gotten out of bed that winter. Although I liked my job, it wasn't enough. Maybe it came down to something as simple as being needed instead of just needy. The paper could get another editor, but who else would put up with Georgia? Who else would love her as much as I did? I put barium shoes on her that winter and rode her through the woods on icy trails where we wouldn't normally go. The shoes held on the ice, and I went farther into the woods than I'd ever gone in winter. I liked that it was so dark and quiet, far from any human being, with just animal tracks to show that other creatures existed. I liked being alone with Georgia, the feeling that for a few hours I had someone special all to myself.

That was the winter I sent Jenny away to be trained. I'd found a good trainer at a stable in Woodstock, and since Jenny would be turning three in the spring, it was time to introduce her to a bridle and a saddle and eventually a rider. For two weeks we left an open horse trailer in the pasture, and twice a day I'd put Jenny's grain bucket in the trailer so she'd have to walk up the ramp and into the trailer to eat. She did it willingly from the first day, and by the time she left two weeks later, she was calm and relaxed for her short trailer ride. Depending on how her training went, she'd stay in Woodstock for at least three months, and I wasn't even sure if I would bring her back after that. A young horse needs to be ridden, and I couldn't ride Jenny every day if I was riding Georgia. Already several people had expressed an interest in taking her, and it was likely that I would let one of them have her.

The day Jenny left, Georgia, Hotshot, and Tempo stood at the gate and whinnied at the disappearing trailer but quickly returned to grazing when they could no longer see it. Georgia had long ago distanced herself from her foal, growing tired of the nursing, playful filly when Jenny was about eight months old. Since then, Jenny had grown much closer to Hotshot than she was to her own mother. So when she left on that February day, it was Hotshot who stayed at the fence the longest to watch his friend depart.

I was sad when Jenny left. It felt like another big hole in my life on top of the hole created by Tim's betrayal. I even considered going to Woodstock to bring her back. I wasn't ready to let her go. I still needed her. But when I rode Georgia, I didn't feel crazy or needy or afraid. I just felt incredibly lucky, as though I was doing something illegal, and if anybody found out, they'd take her away from me. It wasn't right to enjoy something that much, it wasn't right to own something that beautiful. All through the winter, I rode her before work, and on weekends later in the day when the sun was high overhead and sparkled through the icy branches of the hemlocks like a disco globe. When we returned to the barn, I'd run my hands across her thick winter coat feeling for perspiration, wiping her down with a towel if she wasn't completely dry, brushing out the saddle marks, and picking snow or ice out of the bottom of her shoes. She loved the attention — mine as I fussed over her and Tempo's and Hotshot's as they looked on from the center aisle.

One day, as I stood in the barn brushing her down after our ride, I looked across the pond and the back pasture toward High Point Mountain in the distance and realized I had re-created my life at Camp Treetops. Not only had I found the same view I'd had from my tent at Treetops, but I'd built a barn similar to the one at camp and my life revolved around the care of a horse. It was camp that had nurtured my reverence for nature and all living beings, and it was camp where I felt I knew who I was again. And then all these years later, without being aware of it, I had re-created a home as safe and nurturing as Treetops had been to me.

One night in March I went to bed and didn't wonder about anything. Instead, I fell asleep, and when I woke up in the morning and took Georgia on a slushy ride through the melting snow in the woods, I knew we weren't going anywhere. Later I called the realtor and asked her to take the house off the market. We weren't going anywhere because we were already there. We were home. *What was I thinking?* I asked Georgia.

Sometime in late March, Tim called from Colorado. His voice sounded contrite and something else. Desperate? I wasn't sure. I knew only how my voice sounded, clear and angry, without a shred of neediness, because that was gone, purged out of me along with the fifteen pounds and the *For Sale* sign on the front lawn. I was a different person talking to someone from another lifetime. But I wasn't mean; I just wasn't as lost.

I want to come back, he'd said.

Maybe that's what had sounded desperate to me. Or at least desperately funny because I started to laugh.

You what? I said. I couldn't stop laughing.

What's so funny? he asked, already sounding less contrite.

Perhaps my response had been dismissive. Perhaps I sounded more confident than the facts on the ground warranted. Whatever it was, it did the job. I asked him never to call me again. The monster was out of my life and wasn't manipulating his way back in.

When weekends rolled around, I rode Georgia or went skiing and hiking with friends and discovered I didn't need a man to feel OK about myself. It was a big revelation. For twenty years I'd been on the hunt. What else could I call it? Go out, find a man (almost any man would fit the bill), and drag him back to the homestead, and life could begin. If one relationship failed (and with such a low standard for eligibility, they all failed), life stopped until another could be found. Nothing that happened between men counted. I was just treading water. Without a man, there was no Susan. There wasn't a present that mattered, and certainly there wasn't a future until Tim did me the enormous favor of shattering the lie. Not his lie, mine. The lie that men were the answer, the only answer. That without a man, I was less a woman, less human.

As long as I had believed that, it had been true. I was a woman who couldn't think or act independently, a woman who defined herself through a man. It had never occurred to me to be honest with a man, to tell him what I really thought or felt. To do so would have risked losing him. I had been as much a monster as Tim had been, a liar attracting a liar.

It had taken months of staring at the ceiling in terror at night to learn I could take care of myself. Before Tim, I hadn't known that. After Tim, I would never forget it. It was as liberating as not drinking, and for the first time I began to take myself seriously. It required a conscious effort because the truth is I had no idea what I really thought or felt. I had no idea who I really was. I'd been the person in the room least likely to rock the boat. I was so nice. I smiled at everyone and everything. I would have smiled through a stroke.

After a lifetime of censoring myself, it wasn't easy suddenly to become authentic. I'd find myself in a small group, for instance, deciding where to eat lunch, and someone would say, *Well, I feel like a hamburger,* and someone else would say, *No, let's get a salad,* and another would say, *I hear that new Italian place is good,* and I'd be thinking, *Whom should I side with?* In such a situation, there had been too many chances of offending someone to dare assert an opinion. Determining what I felt like eating depended entirely on what someone else felt like eating. When I was alone, the decision was based on what I should eat, almost never on what I felt like eating.

I learned to think and feel for myself in AA, and I did it

by listening. There are probably few places on earth where uncensored thoughts and feelings flow more freely than at an AA meeting. For someone like me, walking into such an environment had been a shock. AA was where I'd learned I wasn't really so placable, that behind the perpetual smile were big bad feelings like hate, anger, envy, and all the rest. I learned by listening to others — particularly the women — speak frankly about things I wouldn't have admitted to a close friend. Week after week, month after month, I listened to people speak the unspeakable. Beth raged about her mother. *She took so many pills, I never knew whether she was going to be dead or alive in the morning. When Dad left, I was the one who always had to call the ambulance, and I was only eleven. I hated her. She stole my childhood. I started sneaking liquor when I was fifteen. It made dealing with my mother easier.*

Mary spoke of debilitating envy of others in her profession. *I was offered the lead role in a sitcom, but I refused to leave New York and move to Los Angeles because of my cat. It was really because of drinking. The actress who got the part is a huge name now. That could have been me.*

Nancy expressed deep shame about a birth defect. *When it's on your face, you can't escape it. I was teased at school and stared at everywhere else I went. I was afraid to leave the house. When I started college, I discovered beer. It was all over after that.*

I listened amazed, first at the honesty and eventually because I discovered it was how I felt or thought, too. I listened to their feelings and looked for mine.

This process of self-discovery took months. *Yes, that's how I see it,* or *No, that's not me.* With twenty or more people at a meeting, I was bound to bump into a part of myself every time I went. For a long time I just listened, and eventually, when I spoke, I'd say things like *I feel the way Judy feels,* or *Boy, I couldn't have said it better than Nancy.* I don't think I uttered an original thought for five years.

AA wasn't the only place I was discovering who I was. Every time I walked into the barn, if I paid attention, I could learn something important about human nature, including my own. For example, I was a lot like Hotshot, who lived in fear of offending Georgia and was grateful to be allowed to blend quietly into the herd. His message was, whatever you want is OK with me. He was sweet but unknowable. Somewhere he had learned that the best way to get along in the world was to keep your mouth shut and to do what you're told. It made living with him easy, but it wasn't a way of life I wanted to emulate. I didn't want the Georgias of the world taking away my choices, dictating my every move. To live like Hotshot meant living with that smile on my face and pretending everything was just fine, always and perpetually fine. I felt sorry for Hotshot sometimes because although he was a genuinely sweet animal, there was a lot more to Hotshot than he felt comfortable letting on. I kept hoping the real Hotshot would show up.

Tempo was the most complicated horse in the barn. He was easier to know than Hotshot because Tempo was completely authentic. He possessed a quiet authority and was the only horse Georgia never challenged. However, like me, Tempo was often anxious, which made him aloof. Better to cock your tail, snort, and flee from the strange new object (a jacket thrown over the fence, a different-colored salt lick, a plastic bag blowing across the pasture, and so on) than to risk being killed investigating. It was life and death for Tempo, every day. If Tempo had been human, he would have built and stocked a bomb shelter in the backyard. He would have prepared for Armageddon. I understood and loved Tempo, but he wasn't a good role model for me either. We had too much in common already.

I was thirty-six going on eight, the same age as Georgia, except she knew exactly what she thought and felt and had no trouble expressing it. She was moody, self-centered, and bossy. As a human, she would have been insufferable, but as an equine, she was an inspiration. It was her confidence I admired. She was never anyone but herself. She didn't apologize and she didn't accommodate. She didn't always get her way, but she always made it clear what she wanted. I remembered the first time I'd heard someone say *No is a complete sentence.* I had mulled it over for weeks, shocked and thrilled by its implications. It had seemed like such an important piece of information; how had I missed it? Georgia said no all the time, and I didn't love her any less for it. I wanted to learn to say no, to wipe the smile off my face, and to eat frosting out of a can if I felt like it.

Between lessons in the barn and lessons in AA, I inched my way toward what I came to think of as *the other me.* The me that was supposed to have been or could have been or should have been. I wasn't sure. I only knew it wasn't possible to remain the same because it was a big lie, and once I knew that, there was no going back. I didn't want to be a liar. The trouble was, there was no one to put in her place, at least no one familiar.

I'd been invited to have dinner with a new friend from AA. I was thrilled because Lauren was an accomplished artist who lived alone on a beautiful farm and obviously knew how to take care of herself, just the kind of woman I admired and wanted to know. We sat in her 1800s kitchen with the big beams and the old trestle table and talked while she cooked, and I reveled in the notion of a new friendship. She told me about the art world in New York City, and I told her about my editing job with the paper. What could have been more pleasant? Two women sharing snippets of their lives with each other in a lovely house filled with the smell of good food.

I'm thinking of getting a couple of horses, she said. *I don't know anything about them, but I hate to waste the barn and all this pastureland.*

Great idea, I said, already imagining how wonderful it would be to have a friend to ride with. *You'd be great with horses.*

I don't know, she said, glancing at me over her shoulder as she sautéed onions. *I've never even been on one.*

You'd learn, I replied. *You're smart and sensitive. You're a natural.*

Stop patronizing me! she said, turning back to the stove and slamming down the wooden spoon.

There was such anger in her voice that my whole body went rigid. If I had been eating, I would have choked. I could hardly breathe. The rest of the night was a blur. I was careful, polite, and terrified.

By the time I drove home, I understood that I had a choice. I could blame Lauren for her crazy outburst, or I could pay attention to what she had said. I ended up doing both. Lauren had been wrong. I hadn't been patronizing her, but I hadn't been honest either. I was playing Hotshot at dinner instead of Georgia, and someone as clear and confident as Lauren had lost patience for such polite insincerity, for an evening of endless deference. It would be months before I could talk to Lauren about that night, months before I could tell her how shy I felt and how anxious I was to make a new friend. She confessed it had been a difficult night for her, too, that she still felt raw and awkward without a drink to get through a social event. It was one of the most honest discussions either of us had had in early sobriety, and with it began our real friendship.

I slept badly the night of Lauren's dinner and woke up earlier than usual the next morning. It was barely light when I threw my leg over the saddle and headed through Henry's fields toward the woods. The air was chilly and damp, filled with the smell of earth and pine. Georgia broke into an easy canter along the rock wall at the edge of the field. Part of me wanted to canter into the woods and never come back, to get as far away from humans as I could, as far from the shadow I'd become in the presence of my own species.

I gripped my horse, feeling her powerful muscles move beneath me, her effortless stride carrying us across the wet grass toward the rock wall separating one hay field from another, a low wide wall about three feet high and four feet across. Every morning I had stopped at this wall, turning right into the woods through an opening and emerging in the next field through a second opening. It wasn't that the wall was too high or too wide for Georgia to jump, it was that the ground dropped about two additional feet at a forty-five-degree angle on the far side, and I wasn't sure I could stay in the saddle on such a steep grade. I imagined myself flying over her head and landing on the ground just in time to be trampled to death as her front feet touched down.

That morning as I approached the wall, for the first time a voice in my head said, *Oh, for God's sake,* and I didn't rein her in. I didn't slow her down. As we cantered closer, I could feel Georgia collecting herself, gathering tight for the launch, and then suddenly we were in the air, her front legs tucked high as I leaned forward over her neck at take-off. In midjump, just before she began the descent, I had one thought: *Throw yourself out of the saddle sideways.* But she overjumped so high and so wide that we cleared the slope entirely, and she hit flat ground at a dead run. We streaked across Henry's field so fast, if people had seen us from the road, they might have thought we were running away from something. They might have thought we were scared. But they would have been wrong because we weren't. Not at all. *Not ever again,* I thought.

{CHAPTER 8}

IT WAS A SATURDAY morning in the late fall of 1988, and I was riding bareback because I was tired and cold and wanted to feel the comfort of Georgia's warmth. She picked her way carefully over the path of newly fallen leaves, never as sure-footed since her bout with laminitis. Still, her step had a spring, and she seemed eager to head into the woods for her first outing in a week. Except when she'd been sick, it was the longest time I'd gone without riding her. I was filled with guilt and concern about her new, more sedentary lifestyle and wondered what it would do to our relationship, as well as to her overall health. Morgans can put on weight easily, and Georgia was no exception. Her grain ration was half of Tempo's and Hot-shot's, and still it was hard to keep her weight down.

She gets fat on air, I said to the vet, who told me Georgia needed to lose at least fifty pounds.

How was I going to get the weight off if I couldn't ride her every day? And how would she behave on the trail after days of not being able to blow off steam? Georgia had never been a sit-around-the-barn kind of girl. She wanted to see what the two draft geldings down the road were up to and if the old lady at the end of the dirt driveway would remember to bring a carrot out for her as we passed. She even wanted to pretend to be afraid of the bridge we crossed every morning, and she definitely wanted to get me wet as she splashed across a shallow part of the same stream farther up the trail.

Riding horses had always been a way to remember who I was in the changing landscape of my life: a good rider. When I was five and numb with grief at the loss of my mother, I discovered that I was a good rider. When I was eight and failing everything in school and facing the rage of a disappointed grandmother, I was a good rider. When I was twelve and living in Baltimore, hostage to a drunken grandfather and a battering stepgrandmother, I remembered I was a good rider at camp. Over the years, it was the one sure thing I knew about myself. It kept me connected to me, the person I was at my core.

I worried about my bad back, running out of money, and Georgia foundering again—all the things that could interfere with riding, ending a lifestyle that felt essential to me. In my drinking life, I had dragged myself to the barn in the morning and galloped off the headache and what-ever craziness still lingered from the night before. I was always riding for my life. Nothing else soothed me in the same way. Nothing else mattered as much. I was bad at relationships—made more difficult still by the shyness that came with being sober—but Georgia was the one being whose eye I could meet with confidence—no small feat for someone who had trouble with eye contact.

I shivered in the cold morning, my eyes still puffy from too little sleep, my head jammed with obligations that left no time for this leisure, if riding could be considered leisure. I'd woken up and gone to the barn anyway, stealing an hour because I knew that if I didn't ride, I wouldn't be able to think about anything else for the rest of the day. If only I hadn't thrown away most of my grandmother's money. If only I'd been able to make ends meet on my salary as an editor. But the new busy schedule was really the result of AA. It was really about growing up and learning to go more boldly into the world. If I still had my grandmother's money, I might never have left Jane Austen and ventured out of the living room. I might never have taken the next big step.

One night after an AA meeting at the local library, a man named Jim approached me as I helped clean up in the kitchen. I'd seen Jim at various AA meetings over the previous two years but had never spoken to him because he intimidated me. He was the director of a residential treatment program for alcoholics, and I paid particular attention when he spoke because he always said something interesting. He was tall and handsome, in his forties, and had been sober for about fifteen years. He'd come and go at meetings, never staying behind at the end to socialize with the others. He'd lost everything to alcohol—his

family, his home, and his job — before pulling himself together and going back to school for a master's degree and
a fresh start.

As he walked toward me, I turned my head to see who
he was coming to talk to, never imagining it could be me.
But when he stopped and leaned against the sink, waiting
for me to finish rinsing out the coffeepot, my confusion
turned into the horrible shyness I experienced in the presence of anyone I didn't know, especially a man.

When you have a moment, I'd like to talk to you, he said.

Was he about to ask me for a date? This was hard to
imagine, but I couldn't think of any other reason he'd
want to talk to me. I'd always stayed away from the men
in AA. The program discouraged relationships in the first
year of sobriety, but also newly sober people are pretty
crazy, so AA never seemed like a smart dating pool to me.
It was hard enough to find safe friendships among the
women. But with fifteen years under his belt, Jim was sort
of a magnum cum laude of AA, and I was flattered that he
sought me out.

He suggested we go outside and sit in a couple of
wicker chairs on the far end of the front porch, where we
could talk without being interrupted. As I followed him, I
wracked my brain for what I would say if he asked me out.
Of all the men I'd met in AA, he was certainly the most
appealing, but I didn't feel ready to start dating again. I
loved my job at the paper and did most of my socializing
with Lane and the others who worked there or with new
women friends from AA. Early mornings and weekends
were reserved for Georgia and the other horses, which
didn't leave much time for anything else. Besides, I loved
the serenity that came with not having a man in my life.

Sometimes I was lonely, but there wasn't much time to be lonely. Tim had been out of my life for almost two years, and I hadn't had a date since. I was just beginning to value my independence.

Have you ever thought of doing counseling work? Jim asked as soon as we were settled.

I'd been so busy planning how to deliver my I-don't-date speech, I was caught completely off-guard by his question.

Counseling?

We need to hire someone to assist in running a women's group at the rehab, and I think you'd be good.

I told him that for the past two years I had been the editor of a small newspaper, before that a customer service manager, and before that a high school English teacher. No counseling experience, unless you counted talking to students about why they weren't doing the work or holding a customer's hand through a product complaint process.

Still, I was interested. I was definitely interested.

You could try it for a few months and see how it goes, he suggested. *Groups meet nights and weekends, so it wouldn't interfere with your job. And you'd get paid.*

I'd gone home and thought about it for a nanosecond before deciding to try it. The more I thought about it, the more I loved the idea. It seemed too good to be true that I'd even been asked. It was one of the few times in my life when I didn't question my own competence. What I didn't know about counseling I could learn. I'd always been an observer, a listener, an empathizer. It was a start. If things worked out, I'd even consider leaving the paper. I was having a hard time living on the salary anyway, and the hours were so long I hadn't been able to find time to start any of the independent writing projects I'd been mulling around for years — that collection of short stories, that novel.

A week later I sat in on my first group, led by a Catholic nun named Sister Gloria. What an eye opener. I don't know which shocked me more, the religious slant of some of Sister Gloria's counseling or the stories the women told about themselves. The experience of both put me so far outside my comfort zone, I wasn't sure I'd be able to continue. I didn't mind when people found strength in their religious beliefs. I minded when religious dogma was imposed. I minded when it was called therapy.

As for the stories the women told, they were so much worse than anything I'd heard in AA, so much worse than my own history of maltreatment, that I wasn't sure I could bear listening to them. Suddenly I felt like a spoiled rich white woman whose biggest problem was figuring out how to spend more time with her horse. My presence in the mixed group of twenty black, Hispanic, and white women, all from New York City, seemed almost obscene. Most of the women had union jobs with the sanitation department or transit authority, who contracted with the rehab to take its members; some were on welfare; and some were street workers and small-time drug dealers. None of them had had a rich granny who'd given them anything. Who was I to think I had answers for these women? Who was I to think I had answers for anyone?

I went home shaken and confused and headed straight to the barn. It was after eleven o'clock on a warm spring night, and the bullfrogs and peepers were in full chorus. The ground was moist and spongy, and the earth smelled fresh and green. I could see the dark shapes of horses in the far corner of the pasture, lit by a bright full moon. I used to ride when the moon was full, especially when there was snow on the ground to highlight the trail through the darkness of the trees. I'd ride bareback and feel Georgia float on the snow beneath me, her breath a ghostly gray plume filling the air around us.

I hadn't ridden at night in a long time, but after that women's group, I went to the barn, grabbed Georgia's bridle, and walked across the pasture to find her. When I did, before I slipped off her halter, I stood with the three of them clustered around me, doling out peppermints and scratching necks. It seemed to me that this was my church, this pasture, this barn, this land surrounded by mountains and forests and streams, and that to live in the perfection of nature, to live with animals is to know the divine. The texts of man seemed clumsy and didactic compared with the wisdom of a tree, a dragonfly, a horse. It was this wisdom, always present but never preached, that I looked to in moments of doubt and despair.

I slipped Georgia's bridle over her head and led her toward the fence to climb up and mount her. She didn't seem worried about the peculiar hour or that Hotshot and Tempo weren't coming with us. After years of riding out alone, her anxiety about separating from the herd had been tempered with the fact that we always came back. She was never separated for long. Still on her, I leaned over and opened the gate, with pressure from my legs guiding her to pivot neatly around the opening, which was just big enough for her to get through without letting the other two out. She did this perfectly, nickering a halfhearted fare-well to Tempo and Hotshot, who leaned over the gate and watched us disappear toward the pond.

The bullfrogs and peepers went silent as we passed, resuming their song only when we were well up the path on the way to Henry's hay fields. Without snow, it was too dark to ride in the woods, but Henry's fields were bright enough to ride across safely, and as long as we stayed near the edge, we wouldn't damage the delicate new grasses just beginning to emerge. I found the opening in the stone wall between my property and Henry's and let Georgia pick her way through the rubble of rocks that seemed to crop up fresh every few months no matter how many times I cleared them away.

The moon was low in the western sky, casting long pale shadows across the landscape dotted with the barns and outbuildings of Henry's farm. His three hundred chickens were quiet in their coop, guarded by a flock of domestic geese as ferocious as any good farm dog. Ferocious enough to stop the school bus most mornings until Henry came down to the road and hustled them away. Georgia refused to walk by when they were there, terrified by the memory of one grabbing her tail and holding on as she cantered to get away. I'd had to dismount and chase the goose off with a stick. Georgia's fear of geese had extended to my own two, and when they sometimes ducked under the fence to nibble at the clover in her pasture, she kept a watchful eye.

There were no geese to impede our way across the fields that night, no squirrels or blowing leaves or snakes or any of the other half dozen or so things that could make her suddenly jump sideways in midstride, once or twice leaving me surprised to find myself on the ground next to her, looking up. She held her head high with ears perked forward, breaking into an easy trot along the edge of the field as if nothing could be more normal than going for a ride in the middle of the night.

I was touched by her trust in me, her trust that wherever we were going, it would be OK because she was with me and I had never put her in danger. Not real danger. She trusted that I knew her and her limitations — what she could or couldn't jump, where she was or wasn't willing to go. I didn't ask her to walk through water when she couldn't see the bottom, when it was impossible for her to know how deep it was. I didn't ask her to squeeze through places that were too narrow or to walk down hills that were too steep. I didn't even ask her to like other horses, because I knew it was pointless for me to try to impose my will on such an immutable element of her character. She trusted me, and the reward for both of us was that she was free to be herself in my presence.

Maybe I needed to learn to trust someone, too, someone like Jim, who had listened to me speak in AA meetings for two years (albeit, not often) and had heard something that made him think I might be good at counseling. Maybe I needed to trust that he saw something in me that I couldn't see in myself — someone who could listen to the pain of others without judgment or blame, someone who wouldn't run away. I needed to trust that Jim had shown me a path and that it wasn't too steep or too narrow or too deep for me to follow. Maybe assisting in the women's group could be the beginning of something else, something even more rewarding than writing for the paper.

I let Georgia slide into an easy rocking-horse canter and knew, in spite of being sickened by some of the things I'd heard, I'd go back to the rehab for another group. How often does someone show up and out of nowhere offer an opportunity that could change your life in ways you never imagined? It had happened with the job at the paper, and suddenly it happened again. It was time to pay attention. Counseling had never made it to the short list of career ideas, but ever since Jim approached me, I felt a growing excitement about it. I'd give it a serious try, and if I wanted to pursue it, I could take some classes. Meanwhile, I'd learn what I could from Sister Gloria, which might include a lot about the Bible.

We circled Henry's fields in the moonlight, the only sound the steady rhythm of Georgia's hoofbeats and the soft, staccato snorts of her breath. I nestled easily in the warm curve of her broad back, cushioned by the large muscles with their extra layer of fat. And if I shut my eyes and let myself exist only in the cocoon of her horsy aroma, I could imagine I was any age, anywhere, doing something that for as long as I could remember had made me feel safe no matter what else was going on in my life. I had never been sure of where I belonged until the first time I sat on a horse, and then I knew. I was five when my grandmother gave me that evil pony named Bunty, whom I adored from the moment she flattened her ears and bit me during our introduction. The hours I spent alone with Bunty were the only hours I wasn't afraid, the only time I really felt my heart open to another being. It didn't matter that Bunty bit and kicked. Somehow I knew not to take it personally. I knew it was just who Bunty was and had nothing to do with me. I could see the truth about a horse, and I knew being near her was where I belonged. And thirty years later, in the soft glow of the moon, I knew it again. I belonged on Georgia and all the places that she could take me.

. . .

A year and a half later, it was the middle of the night again and so quiet the only sounds I heard were my shoes swishing through the grass as I walked toward the barn. I didn't know if the horses were in their stalls or outside grazing. It was 4 A.M., the second week of September, and I had just started the second and final year of a master's program in social work. At 6 A.M. I had to drive three hours to get to my first class at Adelphi University in Garden City, Long Island.

Heavy steps cantered across the field in my direction, and in a few seconds Georgia was almost on top of me, followed by a wild-eyed Tempo and a snorting Hotshot. I handed out carrots and called their names as we jostled together toward the barn, where I entered first, feeling around on the wall for the light switch. All three stood in the entrance, blinking sleepy eyes at the sudden glare, uncertain about what was expected of them. It had been years since they'd been fed at 4 A.M., not since I'd ridden Georgia when I'd been editor of the paper, so no one rushed into a stall, which would have been the usual morning routine. Instead, they lingered in the doorway, waiting to see what I would do. As soon as they heard the heavy wooden lid of the grain bin creak open behind the tack-room door, they clattered down the aisle into their respective stalls, nickering with excitement at the unexpected meal. Tempo pounded the wall with a front hoof, Hotshot walked in quick circles, and Georgia paced up and down the center aisle, pinning her ears at Hotshot every time she passed him.

I fed Georgia first to get her out of the way, Tempo next to stop the pounding, and finally Hotshot, the only one who would tolerate waiting. While they ate, I climbed

Lane's spiral staircase to the hayloft. The contractor had intended to build a ladder fixed to the tack-room wall, but Lane thought stairs would be easier for me. They were an elegant touch in an otherwise standard barn. Every time I used them, I thought of Lane.

I dropped hay through the opening above each stall, knowing it was going to be a warm day, which meant the horses would remain in the cool, dark barn to avoid the heat and bugs. I mucked stalls, picked hooves for pebbles and grit, swept the center aisle, and turned on the fans before I flipped off the lights and walked back to the house across the still-dark pasture an hour later. The horses wouldn't be fed again until nine o'clock that night. It was a terrible routine, but not as terrible as the first year of classes, when I hadn't returned home until ten.

In some ways, it felt that I was losing what mattered to me most. My beloved Bear had just died at the age of twelve. I had watched him hobble across the lawn, arthritic and nearly blind, past the pond and into the woods. It was his daily routine, only the last time he did that I never saw him again. I looked for him everywhere, scouring the woods and the fields for his body. I enlisted Henry's help, and for a whole afternoon, we rode around on his tractor, searching deeper into the woods in every direction. It broke my heart not to have a gravesite to honor the memory of my sweet dog.

In addition to losing Bear, I had all but lost my morning rides on Georgia because I was too tired or too busy. After two and a half years with the paper and six months assisting Sister Gloria, I had left my editorial job so I could work at the rehab center full-time. I helped Sister Gloria with the women's groups; Jim had asked me to develop a lecture series to present once a week to the entire facility. I loved working there, and after paying me a small salary for the first few months, Jim called me into his office and offered a substantial increase if I was willing to get my master's in social work. He would schedule my work hours around classes and personally supervise my field placement. It seemed like a fantastic offer, but I left his office full of doubts. Could I get into graduate school? How would I pay for it? Was thirty-seven too old to begin a new career? Would I have to take *math*? The obstacles seemed overwhelming.

I must have wanted it more than I realized because three weeks later, after borrowing tuition money from my aunt, I was enrolled as a full-time student at Adelphi University's Poughkeepsie campus, an hour's drive from home. (Adelphi allowed students from the Hudson Valley to complete their first year in Poughkeepsie, but we had to attend the Garden City campus the second year.) At the same time, I started a forty-hour workweek as an assistant counselor, which meant that four days a week, I left work at five to attend night classes from six to nine, not returning home to feed the horses until ten. And on weekends I attended additional alcoholism counselor credential classes.

I was never not bone tired. If I hadn't liked the work so much, I never could have sustained the effort. There was an intensity about school that was different from anything else I'd experienced. Social work is the study of human behavior, so there you are, there is your family, unraveled in the harsh clinical glare of a book entitled *Psychopathology* or *Heredity in Health and Mental Disorder.* Suddenly there was a Latin name for that quirky thing your grandmother used to do. There was a medication. No one escaped from social-work school without a self-diagnosis. We were warned not to do this, but everyone did it anyway. I came up with at least four, none of which fell into the "requires hospitalization" category: panic disorder, social phobia, generalized anxiety disorder, and posttraumatic stress syndrome.

Using the *Diagnostic and Statistical Manual of Mental Disorders,* I diagnosed Georgia and came up with four for her, too. According to the manual, she fit the diagnosis of oppositional defiant disorder — *negative, hostile, and defiant behavior.* Or intermittent explosive disorder — *aggressive impulses resulting in serious assaults.* Or histrionic — *excessive emotionality and attention seeking.* Or narcissistic — *a grandiose sense of self-importance.* Bingo!

I concluded there were two kinds of crazy people: the ones who knew they were crazy and the ones who didn't. Those who didn't were the ones you had to worry about. The rest of us were everywhere you looked: in the grocery store, at work, and across the table at dinner. Nobody made it through life without scars; it was just a question of what kind.

Probably no book described my scars better than Alice Miller's *The Drama of the Gifted Child: The Search for the True Self.* In a text combining equal amounts of compassion and psychoanalytic theory (a rare combination in academic writing), Miller laid out the causes and consequences of childhood trauma. I was my own first client, a sometimes frightening prospect. But for the first time, I was able to look at the events and circumstances of my past more objectively. I was able to see the role alcoholism had played across several generations. There were new words to describe what had happened, words that didn't blame. *Disenfranchised, displaced, bereaved, estranged.* It was still a painful childhood, but I wasn't its only victim. There were many, perhaps all of us: children, parents, grandparents, aunts, and uncles, trapped together in the predictably disastrous consequences of alcoholism.

For the first time I felt less dismissive of my family, less willing simply to write them off as monsters, as a group best dealt with by cutting off all contact. I came to see my father in particular (the person I both loved and blamed the most) in a different way. He, too, was the product of an alcoholic father, who had died in a drunk-driving accident when my father was only thirteen. He, too, was raised by the same angry woman who had raised me, and he, too, developed a drinking problem early in life. But my father was also diagnosed as bipolar, a mental illness whose scope and complexity I came to understand more fully for the first time. As the professor put it on the day we began studying the disorder, *Being bipolar is no picnic.*

My father had suffered. It was hard to believe it had taken me so long to grasp this. My angry grandmother had suffered, too, first as the daughter of an alcoholic father and then as the wife of an alcoholic who left her a young widow, and finally as the mother of two alcoholic children. And then in her early sixties, just when it looked like clear sailing for my grandmother, my brother and I were thrown into her life, the product of a dead mother and a disappeared, alcoholic father.

My family had had no language for any of this. If it was discussed at all, it had been behind closed doors with a lot of anger and finger pointing. The men were called weak and the women bitches. Appearances were everything, so secrecy was valued above openness, lies above truth. Under this plan, everybody suffered.

For once I felt like Georgia, someone who had been self-absorbed for so long, she had only just figured out that Tempo had feelings, maybe even Hotshot, too. I was tempted to call up the whole family, a sort of giant conference call, and say, *Guess what? We're not bad, we're alcoholics! There's a treatment for this!*

I called my father for the first time in years and said something to that effect. I don't remember his response, only that nothing much between us had changed. He was still distant and never initiated contact, and I still thought in ultimatums: *If he doesn't call me next time, I'll never call him again.*

I was so tired during graduate school that when I rode Georgia at all, I rode her bareback. I don't exactly know why I started this habit, but after I began school, I hardly ever rode with a saddle again. Georgia was an easy ride bareback, broad and fleshy, with a soft, springy walk and a smooth canter. Her warmth was a comfort, and maybe most of all, without the saddle, we were simply closer. I missed our daily rides. Mornings and nights in the barn felt short and rushed. One of the hopes that sustained me through this period was that when school was finished, I would be able to resume regular riding. I was willing to give it up temporarily, but I was determined to establish a lifestyle that left plenty of time for horses.

One Saturday morning I went to the mall to buy a pair of boots. It was the first time in months I'd been in a big public place besides the grocery store and school. I felt assaulted by the bright lights and general commotion and realized I'd been living too long in the alternate universe of books and papers. I bought the boots and left quickly, feeling overwhelmed and exhausted by the experience.

I met a woman at work who had done exactly what I was doing: full-time school with a full-time job. She told me she used to fall asleep at her desk between seeing clients, at her kitchen counter eating breakfast, and at school during lectures. All the same places it had happened to me. Sometimes at night I dropped across the top of the bed and fell asleep with all my clothes on. Sometimes I never made it upstairs and fell asleep on the living room couch.

It ruined my health, the woman at work had told me.

I felt like it was ruining mine, too. I had a case of strep throat that wouldn't go away. I'd take a ten-day course of antibiotics, feel better, but a week or two later, the sore throat would return and I'd be back on antibiotics. This went on for months.

You need to rest more, the doctor said.

When? There wasn't time. I felt I'd wasted so much of my life already in ten years of alcoholism, two failed marriages, and too many job changes while trying to find work I liked that could support me. Most women my age had children or established careers or both. I was thirty-eight and just starting what felt like the adult portion of my life. I didn't have the luxury of youth to dabble. I didn't even have a savings account.

I pushed through the exhaustion. Some mornings I felt so awful I sat on the edge of the bed and cried. Even that felt like a luxury. If I sat there too long, it cut into what little time I had with the horses. So I'd drag myself to the barn and cry there, leaning against Georgia's neck as she ate, her ears flicking in annoyance. She didn't like a lot of what she might have called cloying physical contact. She especially didn't like being bugged while she ate. I bugged her anyway, needing to take her warmth and smell with me into the day ahead.

Classes were so full of information about humans and human social systems that sometimes I felt overwhelmed. But something I learned outside the classroom had more of an impact on me than anything else.

The eye opener happened in the carpool during the weekly three-hour drive to Garden City in the second year of school. I had become friendly with the three women I commuted with in the first year of school, and we often used the drive to talk about the challenges and problems we faced working directly with clients for the first time. I was upset about something I'd heard in an all-women's group at work that week and had recounted the young client's story of sexual abuse to the carpool. The abuse had involved a dog. It was the first time I'd heard such a graphic description of that kind of animal abuse, and I was so shocked by it that when the group had ended, my knees were shaking as I left. I'd gone back to my office and had questioned again whether I could handle becoming a therapist. What possible response could one offer in the face of such cruelty? All I could think was that I hated people. We were some sort of nightmare species, evolved only in our endless capacity to harm.

I told all this to the carpool and anxiously awaited their response. I was sure they could help me. They could at least share my shock, my horror at the behavior of humans. But that's not what happened. Nobody in the car but me seemed shocked or horrified. Instead, sitting in the back seat, I caught a glimpse of the driver's face in the rearview mirror, a pretty woman my age named Eileen whom I had often admired for her knowledge and insights into the human psyche. She was smiling.

What kind of dog was it? she asked.

I was so surprised by her question I thought I heard it wrong. It reminded me of the sick joke about a client who tells a new therapist that her child has just been killed in a car accident, and the inexperienced therapist asks what kind of car it was. *What kind of dog?*

Well, you know, said Eileen, still smiling and then squirming a little in her seat, *I was just trying to imagine that tongue.*

It was the last thing in the world I expected, a cavalier answer, a roguish grin.

Claire and Phoebe smiled, too, giggling a little as the oldest of us, Claire, a retired pharmacist in her mid-sixties, said, *Well, it is kind of erotic.*

Erotic?

For a few minutes I was so confused I didn't know what to think. That's how long it took me to realize they were right. It was erotic. It was a lot of other things, too, but one of them was definitely erotic. What bothered me was that I was the only one in the car who didn't know that. It didn't occur to me.

The importance of self-knowledge was emphasized over and over again in class and while working with the clinical director of my agency — how important it was to feel all of your own feelings first before you can effectively help someone else. It's called countertransference, but all it really means is that you must recognize the complexity of feelings you have about the client or something the client has said. It means clearing away a lifetime of pat, often polite responses and digging out the truth of a thing, like racism or sexism or homophobia, all kinds of stereo-types and prejudices that many of us claim never to feel but learn that on some level we have, we all have.

So in the process of this purge, in the great closet sweep of our own minds and hearts, we might bump into thoughts like *Catholics are rigid, Alcoholics are bad,* or *Educated people are smarter.* The list goes on and on, all the ways we stay distant, separate, or better than the person sitting across the desk, all the ways we stay safe. A good therapist isn't someone who has resolved all these feelings; she is someone who acknowledges them. Over and over again, as often as they come up.

That morning in the car, I saw how far I was from doing this, how knee-jerk my reactions could still be. How thought-*less,* how feeling-*less.* Nobody in the car thought the abuse wasn't horrible; they just knew that it wasn't *only* horrible. They'd been in touch with their own "bad girl" feelings; they'd been honest.

I struggled through graduate school with the double load of learning the course work while learning who I was at the same time. As a motherless and fatherless child being sent to live with a different relative every two years, it had been essential to learn how to blend in, to accommodate, to be vigilant for cues of anger that often led to violence. It had been essential to hide myself in order to get safely through the day. It hadn't been safe to be authentic, to ex-press thoughts and feelings openly. In a violent, alcoholic home, it wasn't even safe for the adults to do so, much less the children, and even less the unwanted children.

As a child, the first authentic relationship I remembered had been with a horse. Thirty-four years later I still knew who I was around horses. I still felt my heart open easily in their presence. A relationship with a horse felt easier and safer than a relationship with a human. But more and more, I was applying what I knew about horses to what I wanted to know about people and what I wanted to know about myself.

Tell me, I said to Georgia one day, after she'd nipped Hotshot because he was standing too close to me, *do you ever hate yourself in the morning?*

{CHAPTER 9}

IN THE SUMMER OF 1990 I'd been sober for seven years. I was forty years old, I'd just finished graduate school, and I was starting a new job as the only social worker on the staff of a residential treatment program for drug addicts and alcoholics. I stood at the window in my new office and looked down across the wide green lawn to where it dropped into the underbrush, which went all the way to the train tracks that ran along the east bank of the Hudson River. It was a good place to stand in breaks between clients. The train whistled by half a dozen times a day, and there was always a barge or a sailboat to watch making its way along the river. The Catskill Mountains rose into the horizon on the other side of the Hudson and gave anyone in need of some harmless drama a spectacular sunset.

It was the most beautiful office I'd ever had, not something a social worker or a public schoolteacher ever expects. It had a white vaulted ceiling and a working pink fireplace. The desk was in front of the fireplace, and on the other side of the room were a couch and comfortable chairs placed around a coffee table where twice a day, a dozen or so clients would come for group therapy. Across the hall was a private bathroom with old brass fixtures and an enormous claw-foot tub. The bathroom even had its own balcony, which looked down on the heart-shaped front lawn the original owner had designed as a gift for his wife. It was on the third floor of a colonial mansion that was part of a once-private two-hundred-acre estate that included a twenty-horse stone stable with bridle paths crisscrossing the property. But there were no horses at my new job. The stone stable had been converted into a separate treatment center for adolescents, and there was nothing left of the bridle paths except for the occasional footpath between buildings.

I'd left my previous counseling job as soon as I had completed my master's degree about four months earlier because this job paid more, and I needed the money to reimburse my aunt for the tuition. Our clients, hardened addicts from New York City, many of whom faced criminal charges or had been expelled as failures from other treatment programs, came here as a last resort. The irony of placing clients in such a spectacular setting was that in addition to learning how to live without drugs, they learned some interesting new words that came with the house, words like *loggia,* which was the glass-enclosed area off the living room, where the first meeting of the day was held on chairs set up on the imported *Paragon glass* tile floor. Or *pecan parquet,* which described the floor in the rest of the house except in the kitchen, where it was *travertine marble.* Scattered around the house were *sterling silver* light fixtures the clients were expected to polish weekly, and it was difficult keeping cobwebs from forming all over the circular *inlaid* wood ceiling. Sometimes I'd find a client standing still in the front hall looking out the French doors past the *Stanford White* marble sculpture of the little boy playing a flute, across the perfectly manicured lawn toward the Hudson River, and he'd shake his head and say, *How did someone like me end up in a place like this?*

I wondered the same thing. How had someone like me ended up working in a place like that? How had I stayed sober for seven years when so many addicts and alcoholics couldn't? I had a few theories but no real answers. One theory was that I had enough resources such as a college education, my own home, and a few family members I could go to for help if I needed money. I was lucky to have those things when so many I met in treatment didn't. Those three critical resources gave me the ability to be independent.

I also lived in an alcohol-free home, where my resolve not to drink was never tested by the presence of others who were still drinking or using drugs. None of my friends drank, and I never put myself in a situation where the people around me were drinking, like in a bar or a party where I knew the liquor would dominate. During my first few years of sobriety, I was willing to go to extremes to avoid alcohol—all the people, places, and things that might have threatened my commitment.

However, none of those measures would have worked if they hadn't served a larger purpose, my passion for horses in general and Georgia in particular. I couldn't both drink and take care of Georgia. The horse world was as cursed with heavy drinkers as any other—drunken cowboys, tipsy hunt masters, and people from both sides of the fence in the racing world. Alcohol abuse was everywhere, but I was never one of the drunks who could get away with it. I tried to imagine what my life would have been like if I hadn't quit, and I always imagined that I would have died. My liver would have exploded, or I would have aspirated vomit, killed myself in a car wreck, or died in a violent encounter with another alcoholic such as my ex-husband.

No, I wouldn't have survived alcoholism, and I certainly wouldn't have been able to indulge my passion for morning rides on Georgia. AA and other treatment modalities say you have to get sober for yourself, that becoming sober for someone or something else won't last if your commitment isn't to yourself first. I disagree. I don't know for sure if I would have stopped drinking if I hadn't had a love for horses. I remember that when Georgia arrived at my farm in Lake Placid, for the first time in a very long time I had something I wanted to live for, something I wanted to protect. It was only after she arrived that I recognized I had a drinking problem at all. I think caring deeply about something outside yourself is essential to any kind of healing. I have never doubted the vital role horses played in my recovery. I had ended up sober, with a good job in a beautiful setting, in large part because of Georgia.

Still, how did any of us end up somewhere as pretty as this rehab center, as elegant? It was the kind of house where the aesthetics alone could make you feel better. And the idea of drugs? Well, it just didn't have that let's-go-shoot-some-dope feel. Instead, the beauty of the place seemed to instill a kind of fantasy in the clients for what could have been, a nostalgia about the different choices they could have made way back when, and how maybe all this could have been theirs.

Well, in a way it was theirs, sometimes for as long as a year, or however long it took for them to "graduate" from the program. I never liked the word *graduate*. It made recovery sound too much like high school, where you graduated from twelfth grade and never went back as long as you lived. Who could say that about addiction? The truth is, many clients graduated from this drug program only to be shipped back again in a month or two months or a year because recidivism was a common problem, making the big graduation ceremony seem particularly pointless. The idea of graduating from drug or alcohol addiction was just one of the many philosophical differences I had with my new employer, but they needed a licensed social worker to meet JCAHO standards, and I needed a job, so we agreed to disagree. I believed in the medical model of addiction, and they didn't.

If addiction isn't a medical issue, then why do insurance companies cover the cost of treatment? I had asked during my interview.

Best scam going, said the friendly director sitting on the other side of the desk. But he hadn't really wanted to discuss addiction. He had played the piano on a cruise ship before living on the street and shooting heroin for fifteen years. He was typical of the kind of person who was promoted in this agency, a place with little regard for formal education and a lot of regard for how screwed up you used to be, especially if it included hard drugs and prison time. For years, the agency had refused to hire anyone who wasn't a former addict, believing it took an addict to save an addict. But in recent years the state had begun to get finicky about operating licenses, qualified health-care providers, and a lot of other regulations that forced this large worldwide agency to start hiring professionals. I was part of that effort, hired a month earlier to work in their first treatment program based on the medical model — which they didn't believe. They needed someone to write the treatment protocol, which is why they employed a licensed social worker who specialized in addiction.

The best part of the job was the freedom I was given to develop the program. The worst part was everything else. It was shock and awe, the boot camp of treatment modalities, which included lots of yelling and name-calling and forcing grown men and women to face the wall until they could "get honest." I thought it was at best ineffective and at worst cruel. But all that craziness was left behind as soon as a client stepped through the door of my office on the third floor, where he or she participated in more traditional psychotherapeutic practices such as talking and listening. I also introduced several twelve-step programs to the facility, something else that contradicted the prevailing philosophy.

I don't know why my subversive theory about the need for empathy and compassion or that addiction might be an illness like diabetes or tuberculosis was tolerated. But I was left alone on the third floor to do my social worker "thing" and was left out of whatever happened on the first and second floors. I felt like my office was Radio Free Europe in the heart of North Korea, as though I was spreading the truth in a repressive, tyrannical regime. I thought I was the voice of reason. At least I wanted to be. Clients were conniving dirt bags on the first and second floors and patients with a serious illness on the third. I worried about the mixed messages but felt exposure to another point of view was better than nothing. So I stayed.

Working there reminded me of living at my grandmother's house in Aiken, South Carolina — not the architecture, but the feel of the place, the world it had occupied, complete with its servants' quarters and the matching minimansion workers' cottage. It reminded me that a house could be heartbreakingly beautiful, yet provide no sanctuary for its inhabitants.

I have just turned six when I arrive at my grandmother's house in Aiken after a three-day drive from New York. I am so carsick, I can barely hold up my head, but even though I am still weak and wobbly when the car pulls off the highway and onto the little road that leads to Aiken, I can see we are going someplace special. We turn again, and the road narrows and becomes red clay. Grandmother explains that the trees growing down the middle of the road are live oaks left there to provide shade for horseback riders.

We drive by houses that look like castles and long white fences with sprawling stables beyond. It is a few days after Christmas, but it is warm enough to roll down the window and smell the pine trees and horses. It feels as if we have driven into a story, a book about a faraway place where everything is beautiful and everyone is happy. I wonder if I will be happy there, too, if I will be safe.

We're here, Grandmother announces as Franz drives through a large wooden gate and onto a circular white-pebbled driveway. And there is her house, a redbrick castle partly hidden by growing vines and still-green shrubbery. Franz and the cook get out of the car and shake hands with a tall man and a heavyset woman wearing an apron, who are standing on the front steps of the house with two skinny little boys beside them.

Mr. and Mrs. Mosley with their sons, JB and Glen, Grandmother says before Franz helps her out of the car. *They take care of the house.*

When we're all out of the car, the Mosleys greet my grandmother, but nobody shakes her hand. The youngest boy clings to his mother, too shy to talk, but the older one smiles and says hello. They have heavy southern accents, something strange and new, which adds to the feeling that I am now in another world. Suddenly Mrs. Mosley sweeps me against her apron and hugs me hard, smoothing my hair and telling me how pretty I am. It has been so long since I've been hugged, since I've been fussed over, that I let myself fall against her, pressing my face into the kitcheny smell of her apron.

Later I run barefoot with JB and Glen across the road and into the Hitchcock Woods, down the wide sandy bridle paths that wind through the three-thousand-acre pine pre serve. We don't care that I live in the big house with the formal garden and the brick walkways and that they live in the much smaller house attached to the stables. We don't care because we love the feel of the sand under our feet and the sound of the wind whistling through the pines.

Later still, JB and Glen help me catch Bunty, the Shetland pony my grandmother has just given me.

You'll need to feed and groom her every day, says my grandmother, leading a fat white pony out of her stall and into the paddock. I don't know which is more surprising: watching my grandmother walk across the dusty paddock in her good shoes or being told this horse is mine.

She hands me the lead line and I wait, expecting her to tell me what to do, but instead she brushes the dust from her hands and walks out of the paddock, closing the gate behind her. I watch her walk up the brick path toward the house and disappear around the corner. I stare at my pony, thrilled and scared because I have fallen in love, but I don't think my pony feels the same way. Her ears lie flat back on her head, and even though I don't know anything about horses, when she weaves her head and lunges for my arm, I know I'm not about to be kissed.

Later, when I return from the doctor's office with a bandaged arm, I go back to the paddock with a bag of carrots, determined to make friends. Bunty seems pleasant enough as long as I feed her carrots, but when the bag is empty, I notice her ears begin to go flat, only this time I know what it means. I grab her halter just in time to keep the flashing teeth away and give her a stern *No!* We are both surprised at the sound of my voice, but it works and she doesn't bite me again. Instead, she spins around, and before I fully understand the new threat, a small black hoof whizzes past my ear.

For some reason I don't hate her. On the contrary, the only joy I know while living with my grandmother is when

I am in the presence of this pony. I learn how to avoid being bitten or kicked and spend almost every waking moment at the stable.

When JB and Glen go with me to catch Bunty, she runs to the far side of the pasture the minute she sees us coming. We fan out, each of us enticing her with a carrot, which eventually wins her over. Then we put on her halter and lead her around the outside of the garden wall to the stable, where we brush her until there isn't a speck of dirt on her pure white coat.

After that we lead her to the fence where, one at a time, we climb to the top rail and slide a leg over until all three of us are sitting on her bareback. With no saddle or bridle, we have no control over where she goes, but we don't care because we just love sitting on her. JB and I are the oldest at six, so we put Glen, who is five, between us in case Bunty bolts. Sometimes all three of us fall off at the same time, and sometimes one of us is left clinging as she bucks herself across the paddock.

I spend more time at JB and Glen's house than I do at my own. It is a three-room brick building across the driveway, behind the garage and attached to the stable. There are three beds crammed into the one small bedroom and a big couch and a television in the living room. After dinner, all of us crowd together on the couch to watch television, and Mr. and Mrs. Mosley hold hands.

In the afternoon, Mrs. Mosley is usually in her small kitchen, stirring big pots filled with things I've never heard of: chitterlings and maw, black-eyed peas, cornpone, and squirrel dumplings. In the morning she comes to Grandmother's house to clean and to put fresh flowers in all the rooms. Mr. Mosley fixes whatever needs fixing around the property, but he always goes home for lunch. Before he eats, he gives Mrs. Mosley a big hug hello, lifting her off her feet until she screams at him to put her down. Of course, she isn't really mad. They never say anything mean to each other, and they never yell at JB or Glen or me, even when we do something wrong, like the time we let Bunty out of the paddock and Mr. Mosley had to run down the road to catch her.

Grandmother hires someone named Mr. Newman to come to the house five mornings a week and give me riding lessons on Bunty. He arrives on his horse, Blind Date, a dappled gray thoroughbred whose hooves make a nice crunching sound as they trot across the pebble driveway. The first time Mr. Newman comes, he teaches me how to bridle and saddle Bunty by myself so I will be ready and waiting in the driveway when he comes again. After that, I am never late for my lesson, and we leave Grandmother's house together and head across the road into the Hitch-cock Woods.

Mr. Newman likes to talk about the South and how people from the North just don't understand, and especially how they don't understand how to ride. He has a south-ern accent and calls me Miss Richards, which no one has ever called me before, not even Grandmother's drunken black gardener, Willie, who calls me Miss Susan. Willie comes to the house every day, bringing a whole truckful of rakes and clippers and wheelbarrows, but mostly he finds a shady bench in the garden and falls asleep. Later, Grand-mother will wander around the brick paths, and when she spots Willie, she will wake him up and make him come into the kitchen to get something to eat. She never yells at him for sleeping or for smelling of whiskey or for not doing a lick of work.

Willie, she says, shaking her head, *nobody understands plants the way you do.*

Mr. Newman says Bunty's bad behavior is my fault, and if I want her to change, I have to change. I think about this a lot, wondering what terrible thing there is about me because Bunty bites and kicks and seems to hate everyone. If we walk behind Blind Date, she nips at her hind legs, and if we walk in front of her, she kicks. Mr. Newman makes me put a red ribbon on Bunty's tail so everyone knows it isn't safe to stand behind her.

Still, even with the biting and kicking and wondering why I am such a terrible person, I love riding more than anything in the world, and I love Bunty. And though Mr. Newman says most people from the North can't tell one end of a horse from another, we go for longer and longer rides, and pretty soon we're cantering side by side down the wide sandy trails, and Mr. Newman says it's time I have a proper riding jacket for horse shows.

One day Lloyd comes home. His boarding school is only a few miles away on the other side of town, but this is the first time Grandmother has allowed him to visit. I haven't seen him for almost a year, and he seems old and quiet. He hardly talks to me and isn't interested in meeting Bunty or hearing anything about my rides with Mr. Newman in the Hitchcock Woods.

A few days after Lloyd comes home, it snows, and Lloyd and I meet JB and Glen in the bamboo forest behind the garden wall and build a scraggly-looking snowman together. It is the first time Lloyd seems like his old self, and he laughs and talks as if we've never been apart. After that, the four of us are always together except during my riding lesson, and Mrs. Mosley says it does her heart good to see a brother and sister together the way God intended.

Then Lloyd goes away again. Franz drives him back to school after breakfast one morning, and the house is so quiet I want to run away. Instead, I go to the stable, and for the first time I take Bunty out by myself and ride alone into the Hitchcock Woods. I don't know what she will do when there is no one around to bite or kick, and at first she does nothing, trotting down the path with her ears forward as if she has never in her life had a single evil thought. I do all the things Mr. Newman has taught me to do — heels down, knees tight, hands level, and back straight — and I think I must be changing and becoming a better person because Bunty does everything right, too.

I don't have a watch, but I know I've been riding for a long time because I start to get hungry. Bunty must be hungry, too, because more and more she pulls at the reins, trying to grab a bite of leaf every time we pass a tree that isn't a pine. Ordinarily she doesn't do this, so as I am thinking about turning around and going back, Bunty suddenly bucks and rears, throwing me out of the saddle and over her head, and I land face-down in the sand. By the time I get up and brush the sand out of my eyes, Bunty has spun around, and I just catch my last sight of her red tail ribbon as she canters around the corner, heading for home.

I start walking. There are trails all over the place in every direction, and I never pay attention to whether I am going left or right or straight, especially when I am with Mr. Newman, as he makes all the decisions. For the first time, at every intersection I have to decide which way to go, and

I have no idea except to look for Bunty's hoof prints in the sand. The trouble is there are lots of hoof prints, and I'm not sure which ones are Bunty's and which are someone else's. Bunty's are small, so when I see small hoof prints, I follow those and hope I come out in the right place.

Hours go by, and I am very tired from walking in the sand. My feet sink with every step I take. It is like walking down an endless beach, except there is no water. It never occurs to me to be afraid, to think I will be lost in the woods forever because these are the Hitchcock Woods and I've never been happier anywhere in my life than I am right here. I'm tired and I'm hungry, but I'm not afraid. Not for a minute.

Just when it begins to get dark, I see a man walking down the path toward me. He is tall and skinny and is wearing blue jeans and a sweatshirt. When he comes closer, I see that it is Mr. Mosley, and I start running toward him. Behind him are JB and Glen. When I reach them, Mr. Mosley picks me up and throws me into the air.

Where you been, girl? He laughs, putting me down and ruffling my hair.

Mr. Mosley holds my hand, JB and Glen throw their arms around me, and we walk together the rest of the way out of the woods.

I practically live at the Mosleys' house, and because of this, I hardly ever see Grandmother or Franz or the cook. I eat breakfast alone with Grandmother in the dining room, but if I eat everything on my plate and don't slouch and don't chew with my mouth open and say *please* and *thank you,* I can leave as soon as I am done, and I don't have to see her again until dinner. After dinner Grandmother goes into the living room to read or knit, and I am supposed to go to my room to do the same, but instead I sneak back to the Mosleys' and watch television. If Grandmother finds out, well, that will be the end of that.

One Sunday night at dinner, after we've been in Aiken for a few weeks, Grandmother announces that I am to start school the next day. When we left Rye, I was in first grade, and Grandmother says I will continue in first grade in Aiken. I don't know why I am so shocked to hear that I will be going back to school. I thought I was just going to ride Bunty and play with JB and Glen forever. Grandmother sees the surprise on my face and tells me that JB will be going back to school, too, because Christmas vacation is over.

The idea that I'll be going to school with JB helps ease the shock. *Will Franz drive me and JB to school together?* I ask.

Don't be ridiculous, she says.

The next morning Franz drives me alone to a small white building that looks like someone's house and drops me off at the front gate.

Twenty or so children, all different ages, play on the big front lawn, but no one speaks to me, so I walk down the path and up the steps to the front door and go inside, right into a classroom filled with rows of wooden desks. There are a few more children inside, coloring or playing with puzzles and games, and the teacher is sitting at a desk in the front of the room. When she sees me, she comes to where I am standing by the front door. She says her name is Mrs. Marsh and that she will be my teacher. She puts her arm around my shoulder and, with a southern accent, tells me which desk is mine and where I should hang my coat. Then she takes me to a storage room where there are stacks of books and supplies and gives me everything she says I'll need. She helps me carry them back to my desk, and by the time we are there, I know she doesn't like me.

You're the only one from New York, she says, smiling. *But here in the South we're friendly to everyone.*

Mrs. Marsh isn't the only one who doesn't like me. By recess I know that Patsy Gooding is the most popular girl in the school. She is not one of the oldest, but she is the one everyone wants to play with. I see her at recess in the middle of a laughing group standing near the swings. Every once in a while Patsy looks at me and says something to the group, and they all laugh. I know they are talking about me. When Patsy looks at me, I smile but she doesn't smile back, and then suddenly she turns and walks toward me, with everyone else following.

When she is standing right in front of me, instead of saying something to me, she makes an announcement to the group. *If anyone talks to her,* she says, pointing her finger at me just inches from my face, *then you won't be able to talk to me.*

For a moment I am afraid she is going to hit me, but she drops her hand and, with one final dirty look, turns her back on me and walks away. Everyone follows, and I am alone on the bench with my heart pounding in my ears. The rest of the day is horrible, but especially lunch, which I spend alone on the same bench, eating an egg-salad sandwich on whole wheat bread with lots of lettuce, which I don't like but Grandmother makes me eat because it is healthy. Sometimes, if no one is looking, I can throw these sandwiches away, but today I am the centerpiece of hate, and everyone is looking to see what I will do.

I am trying not to cry, which makes eating a sandwich

difficult. I take small bites so I won't gag and so I can make the sandwich last for the whole lunch period because if I'm not eating a sandwich, what am I supposed to do?

The minute school is over, I run down the path and out the gate to where Franz is supposed to be parked at the curb, but his car isn't there. I look up and down on both sides of the road crowded with cars, but not one of them is the gray station wagon that belongs to my grandmother. I am desperate to get away from the rush of children talking and laughing their way down the path to the cars, fearful of what they will say to me out of earshot of Mrs. Marsh. I pretend I have forgotten something inside and walk toward the school, but instead I go around the side of the building to the back where I will be out of sight. I wait until all the children are gone, and then I come out of hiding and walk to the swing set on the front lawn to wait until I see Franz's car.

I swing on the swings, holding back tears, afraid that if Franz sees me crying, he will find out why and say I deserve it because nobody likes a prima donna. I swing and swing, wondering why he doesn't come and if somehow he already knows I am hated and has decided to leave me here as a punishment. Mrs. Marsh is still in the school. I know because there is one white car left in the road, and it must be hers. I don't want her to see me crying either, so I think about riding Bunty as soon as I get home, and that helps stop the tears.

Suddenly I hear a car door slam, and there is Franz, standing on the lawn, yelling who do I think I am for keeping him waiting like that and he will never, *ever* pick me up at school again. He continues to yell as I run across the lawn, but it is in German and I can't understand what he is saying as I duck under the swinging hand and run into the road, wildly looking around for the gray station wagon.

Where is it? I say, crying now but not caring what he thinks because I am so confused and frightened.

Where do you think? he barks, pointing to the white car, the only car left on the whole street. And that is how I find out my grandmother has bought a new car.

Going to school scares me, and coming home to Grandmother and Franz scares me, too. I can't see the Mosleys after dinner anymore because Grandmother makes me sit in the living room and read after Mrs. Marsh has told her I am a poor student. I don't mind reading, but sometimes Franz comes in and talks to Grandmother as if I'm not there.

No one will play with such a stupid girl, he tells her, shaking his head.

She makes no effort, Grandmother declares.

And spoiled with such a pony, he says. *I hed nothink vhen I grew up!*

Lily gets straight As and has so many friends, Grandmother points out about a cousin.

And such scuff marks! She won't pick up her feet? Vhat do you expect with such a father? Franz says, shaking his head.

He never should have had children. What on earth was he thinking!

At night I lie in bed and imagine the farm my father is going to buy so Lloyd and I can live with him. During the day I feel dead tired but go to school and ride Bunty as if nothing is wrong. Sometimes I'm so tired I fall asleep at my desk, and Mrs. Marsh yells at me to wake up. Sometimes I fall asleep in the car on the way to the outdoor market with Grandmother, and she lets me sleep while she shops for fresh eggs and real cream. Sometimes I fall asleep in the middle of the pasture, and Mr. Mosley has to come and carry me back to the house. Nobody says anything about the strange sleep, but whenever Mrs. Mosley sees me, she hugs me hard and tells me everything's going to be all right. And even though Mrs. Mosley is the kindest person I've ever met, I know she's wrong and that everything will never be all right.

Aiken was where I learned it was safer to be around a horse who bit and kicked than the humans charged with my care. It's where more than thirty years later I would look back and understand for the first time that the strange lethargy that began while I lived in Aiken was something called clinical depression. And as crazy as it sounds, Aiken is where I first began to dream of finding Georgia, a red round horse with a wavy mane who could dance me back to life.

The agency I was working for was well known for its beautiful campuses all over the world, frequently buying up private estates like the one where I worked. In addition to their eye for good architecture, the other thing they got right was their love of dogs. As soon as a new facility opened, the director would make a trip to the local pound to select a canine. The philosophy behind this practice was never clear to me, but it didn't matter; the sight of a dog weaving through outstretched hands during group therapy was enough of a reason for me.

Our puppy arrived one morning with the facility secretary, who had seen a sign on her way to work advertising free puppies. In spite of lofty claims about its breeding by the litter's owner, the puppy's lineage was indeterminate. But it didn't matter; at ten weeks, she was five pounds of mostly white fluff with some brown markings, and the clients and staff fell in love with her. The privilege of naming her was left to the clients, who after much consideration came up with the unfortunate name of Pilgrim because she had been born on Thanksgiving Day. Within minutes, everyone was calling her Pilly, another unfortunate choice given the nature of our work. I suppose it could have been worse. Dopey? Cokey? Or my favorite, Kahlua?

But Pilly it was, and she became the darling of the facility. Her care was rotated among the clients, and she was always with one of them until one day she broke her leg jumping out of a pickup truck. After thousands of dollars spent on surgery and setting the compound fracture, the facility director decided to euthanize her because her medical expenses were too high. I couldn't afford the medical bills either, but there was no way I would let this beautiful dog die. So I agreed to take her and assume the expenses as long as I could bring her to work with me every day.

Pilly came home to three horses and my Siamese cat, Bosco. She was fascinated by all of them, and as soon as her cast came off, she hobbled around to go nose to nose with each herd member and the cat. Her introduction to equine dining was funny to watch. She seemed both confused and fascinated whenever she saw the horses eat hay. She'd sit a few feet away with her worried, wrinkled brow, watching them pull in mouthfuls of the dry greenish stuff. Her idea of tasty was something more savory: a good chunk of manure, especially if it was still warm, or a crescent-shaped clipping that the farrier had trimmed off the hoof. While the farrier trimmed, she'd stand under the horse until a clipping dropped, and then she'd grab her prize from the barn floor and scurry away to dine in contentment.

Pilly and I soon settled into a routine, going back and forth to work five days a week. She'd stay in my office all day, except when a client would carry her out for a walk. But on the weekends, when we were home, we started to have problems. After her leg healed, she'd wander farther and farther from the house. At first it was just to visit my closest neighbors, but as the months went on, she'd go much farther. I'd never had a dog who wandered, so I had never needed a fence. But Pilly didn't just wander; she left. Once I answered a call from a bicyclist whom Pilly had followed for seventeen miles. I knew, because I clocked it in the car when I picked her up. She wandered so far and so often, she began to lose weight. She had never been an eager eater, but now she hardly ate at all. I tried to watch her, but it did no good. She'd sneak off the property, and hours later I'd get a call from people miles away that she was crying at their back door. I felt guilty, as though something I was doing was driving her away.

Pilly also seemed sensitive to touch, often appearing to be in pain when brushed or petted. Finally I took her to the vet. I explained about the wandering and her poor appetite. A new vet happened to be visiting from Albany that day, a specialist in autoimmune diseases whom my regular vet called into the examination room for a consultation. Many tests later, they concluded that Pilly had lupus and put her on steroids. The high dose immediately restored her appetite and decreased her sensitivity to touch. Within a few weeks her weight was normal, and she stopped running away. She would have to remain on steroids for the rest of her life, but over time I was able to keep her comfortable on a very low dose.

It was impossible to know how long a life span Pilly would have, so from the beginning, I assumed the worst. She might have a year or she might have ten. I didn't know, so I let her eat anything she wanted. This included pizza, ice cream, cookies, chicken nuggets from fast-food restaurants, potato chips, and anything else we might bump into while doing errands around town. She loved riding in the car, knowing that no matter where we went, there would be a treat for her. Fortunately, she never became fat.

She grew to be a lovely seventy-pound dog with a long white coat and brown markings. I'd say she had a good bit of collie in her, with a dash of Lab, Saint Bernard, and Husky. She was a good horse dog, keeping a respectful distance but coming with me to the barn in every kind of weather and developing almost an obsession for hoof clippings the day the farrier came. This was in addition to her daily fare of horse manure, which every dog loved.

On weekends, when I rode Georgia, Pilly followed, her pronounced limp always a concern. But whatever discomfort she felt, it wasn't enough to override her love of trekking through the woods with us. More and more, I only walked Georgia anyway, forgoing gallops and jumping because of increasing discomfort in my back. I'd been ignoring my back pain for years, but it had grown worse, bad enough that during the last visit to my doctor she had suggested I stop riding altogether. My chiropractor had offered the same advice. But not riding was as hard to imagine as not eating.

And then there was Georgia to consider. What would happen to her if I stopped riding her? Hotshot and Tempo were much older and semiretired. But Georgia was only thirteen and needed to be exercised. She'd get bored and fat. She'd miss me. It was bad enough that I didn't ride every single morning anymore. I had almost an hour's commute to work, and there wasn't always time. Besides, I was too tired to keep waking up so early, exhausted from the two-year grind of working and going to school full-time. But I couldn't give up riding entirely, either. Instead, before every ride, I'd take a couple of ibuprofen, give Pilly an aspirin, and off we'd go, a couple of gimpy girls gritting our teeth for a habit I couldn't break. Who was I if I didn't ride?

I was forty years old and for the first time in my life felt like I was on solid ground. Things weren't perfect, but compared with any other time, they were close to it. I had work I loved, good friends who felt more like family than my real family, beloved equine, canine, and feline children, and a home that still lifted my heart whenever I walked through the front door. I'd been sober for almost eight years, enough time to get my marbles back and to start using them. I was less anxious, less shy, and less insecure.

On weekend mornings I'd sit at the kitchen counter drinking coffee, looking out at the pond in one direction and the horses grazing in another, and think, *Is this what happiness feels like?* I wasn't sure. Certainly I had moments when I could say I felt happy. Mostly they happened when I was around my animals or in the presence of a client who was making progress in recovery. But between those moments, I lived with a pervasive sadness, a sort of existential angst I couldn't shake. I was beginning to feel lonelier, too, even though I had chosen solitude as the only real guarantee for peace of mind. I didn't want conflict in my personal space anymore. Even the voices on television felt too aggressive, so I didn't own one. It was NPR or the sound of wind. Anything else felt like an assault.

I thought that by eliminating chaos from my life I would be safe and therefore happy. Maybe that's why I was so neat. If everything was in its place, so was I. So was the world. A neat house was proof that I was in control. A messy house said Armageddon was imminent. The truth is, no matter what I did, I still hadn't figured out how to have inner peace. Riding Georgia was about as close as I could get to it, but even then my morning rides were often spent fretting about one thing or another — like growing old or dying alone or never making peace with my past, whatever that meant. I didn't know. I thought moving away, cutting all ties, and starting over would be enough. Out of sight meant out of mind, until one day I received a phone call from a doctor at Norwalk Hospital in Connecticut.

{CHAPTER 10}

I HARDLY KNEW my father, so when I received the call in November that he was dying, I was surprised that it still mattered to me whether he lived or died. I hadn't had any communication with him for more than five years, and so little for the ten years before that I could count our encounters on one hand. I had collected a list of facts about him over the years and kept them in my head, hoping that someday they might add up to a feeling that I knew him. He didn't like horses; he'd gone to Princeton; he was a World War II bomber pilot; he'd married someone else before he married my mother; he married three more times after she died; he drank away his family, his job, and his money; twenty years later he stopped drinking long enough to replace the fortune he had lost (something to do with math and electronic calculators); he could be the funniest person in the room or the angriest or the smartest or the messiest or the craziest. He was very tall.

When I was four, he had his own plane and took my brother and me up for a ride. I sat in the back seat feeling sick to my stomach, hating everything about it because already I didn't trust him. Another vivid memory before he disappeared from our lives was of him walking down a busy road to look for me after I'd run away. I had filled a baby carriage with my stuffed animals and favorite books and had walked down our road, turning onto a much busier one, heading for my new life. I don't remember why I was running away, what incident had made me decide I had a better shot of living on my own than with my parents. But my father was a full-blown alcoholic by then, and I can only imagine the atmosphere in the house—at the very least there would be my mother's disappointment, if not her anger or worse. I wasn't allowed to leave the backyard for a long time after that, a harsh punishment for someone who was desperate to get away.

Before I left for the hospital, I was so nervous about seeing what my dying father looked like, for the first time in years I wanted a drink. Instead I went to the barn and left a note about feed and hay for my barn help, and then I crosstied Georgia in the center aisle and started to brush her tail. It swept to the ground in tangled shades of red shot through with gold and strawberry highlights. Working on a horse's tail is like playing with the hair of some über-doll—the ultimate Barbie, with tresses so thick and glossy it could have been dreamed up only by Mattel.

When I was eight or nine, I learned how to brush a horse's tail without pulling out a single strand of the precious hair. You start with one ropy tangle, and with bare hands carefully untangle one hair at a time until one section is tangle free, and then you start on another. It can take hours, and only then do you begin using a brush. Even with the brush, you focus on one small section at a time, always starting at the bottom and holding the rest of the tail tightly so you won't dislodge a hair. You treat the mane and forelock in the same way, and after years of grooming this way, you have a horse with thick, gorgeous hair. You also hope that when you're finished, the beautifully groomed horse doesn't bolt and roll the minute you let her go.

I didn't have time to untangle Georgia's tail by hand, so I worked in small sections from the bottom up, brushing in hard, fast strokes that worsened my shoulder, perpetually sore from years of shoveling manure. Georgia stood quietly, enjoying the attention, while Hotshot and Tempo watched from the barn entrance. I should have been packing my suitcase and driving to Connecticut, but the thought of doing that made me sick with anxiety. It had been a long time since I'd felt so unhinged. Part of me was surprised by the strength of the feelings my father's imminent death kicked up, and part of me was surprised I was surprised. I was a social worker, someone who spent her days tramping around the labyrinth of the human psyche. I should have known his dying would matter.

Several hours later, I joined my brother in the visitors' lounge of the hospital, and after we spoke to the doctor, we walked into the intensive care unit together. I was so anxious, I wasn't sure I'd be able to see him. I kept telling myself to take deep breaths, to put one foot in front of the other. I was terrified. It was a knee-jerk reaction to something so old I'd lost any conscious connection to it. It was beyond reason. It was primal. Hospitals meant one thing to me: death. The only thing that kept me together was the desire not to embarrass myself.

My father was lying on his back, hooked up to a dozen tubes and monitors, still conscious. He was intubated, so he couldn't talk, but he raised his hand and waved when he saw us. It seemed absurdly normal, his long freckly arm waving from across the room, as though he waved to us all the time, as though seeing us was routine. We both waved back, and then we were at his bedside, close enough to smell how sick he was, close enough to hear what dying from emphysema sounded like. He barely acknowledged my brother, but he seemed happy to see me. I don't know how I knew. I don't think he smiled. I just felt his relief when I entered the room. I felt his joy.

Right away he indicated he wanted to write something, so I found paper and pen and gave them to him.

Am I dying? he wrote in a shaky scrawl.

That wasn't what I had expected. I thought he would ask for a painkiller or an extra blanket. I was shocked at how quickly he had gotten to the point. But then the father I remembered had rarely minced words.

No. I shook my head vigorously. *The doctor said the ulcer has stopped bleeding. You're out of danger.* That was true. He wasn't going to die from a bleeding ulcer. But his lungs. He'd been smoking four packs of unfiltered cigarettes a day since he was a teenager. Now he was seventy-three.

It was a miracle he could breathe at all. *Your lungs are still a problem,* I added, as if he didn't know. He'd been using oxygen for the past ten years.

He nodded. He knew. He understood. Then he wrote something else.

Portable radio?

My father was a news junkie. He read the *New York Times,* the *Wall Street Journal, Barron's,* the *Financial Times* of London, and his local paper every day. At home the television was always on, tuned to one of the twenty-four-hour-a-day news stations, and in the car it was NPR, unless music was playing, and he'd turn the radio off. I knew because that was the way it was twenty years ago, and my brother, who still talked to him, said nothing had changed.

I had lived with my father and his last wife, Betsy, the year after I graduated from college. I'd accepted his invitation to live with him until I decided what to do next because I had no idea where to go or what to do after I graduated. It was the kind of transition that paralyzed me with indecision and fear. The same thing had happened the summer I was too old to go back to camp and again when I graduated from high school. So after college, I'd driven across the country in my beat-up old Buick and had arrived at my father's house with trash bags as luggage to begin to find out who he really was for the first time. It didn't take long — less than a week — to discover he was smart and moody and maddening, but since I had no place else to go, I stayed. It was 1972, the summer Richard Nixon's presidency fell apart and the summer I really started to fall apart, too, drinking more and more to survive the vicissitudes of living with someone as crazy as my father.

I found a job running a day-care center at a local tennis club where mothers dropped off their children while they took tennis lessons. I'd never been around young children before and wasn't even sure I liked them. I certainly didn't know the first thing about amusing them for the hour or two in which their mothers were gone. The only thing I could think of doing was reading to them, but since their ages varied so much, the older ones would look bored and the little ones would cry, and work was pure chaos. I hated the job because I felt I was so bad at it, and I felt guilty because I thought anyone who didn't like children, especially a young woman, must be a monster. There was a lot of screaming and crying at work, and then I'd go home and there'd be screaming and crying there, too, as Betsy struggled to live with a man who I knew in my heart had been impossible to live with for as long as I could remember. No wonder I'd tried to run away when I was four.

My father had been a news junkie then, too, and, I think, the only person in America who after Watergate still believed Richard Nixon was a good president. My father was the most conservative Republican I'd ever met; he even showed me an early 1950s letter he'd received from Joe McCarthy thanking my father for his support in the work McCarthy was doing to purge Hollywood and other places from Communists. Now, in 1991 and on his deathbed, my father's imagination was captured by Desert Storm, and if he had to die, he would die listening to the coverage about the Gulf War.

I told him we'd bring him a radio later, and then I asked if he was cold, if he was in pain, if he was scared. He shook his head no to all of them. I asked him if there was anyone he wanted us to call, anyone he wanted to see. He shook his head no again. I asked him if he needed help making medical decisions, and if so, did he want me to help make them. He nodded.

Through all of this my brother stood farther from the bed and remained silent. I could see he felt uncomfortable, but I wasn't sure why. When we were little, around the time my mother died, I had been our father's favorite. Not the real favorite, just the child my father didn't hate. Hate was reserved for my brother. I remembered the cruel teasing and the constant criticism, but worst of all I remembered the disinterest. Then, after years of not seeing our father at all, my brother and I had begun to see him again when we were in our early twenties, but the pattern of criticism and sarcasm toward my brother had resumed.

In my early thirties, all that changed. When my marriage ended, my father was angry that I had lost Grandmother's money and the house. Never mind that I was a full-blown alcoholic; to him it was the money that mattered. He couldn't believe I'd put the house in my husband's name. He couldn't believe I'd spent a year fighting for a horse and not for the house or the money. After that, Lloyd became the good son. My father would call him up and rant about his sorry sister. He belittled everything I did: my job as an editor, my going back to school for a master's, and finally my career as a social worker, even my sobriety, making fun of AA. He dismissed my expressed desire to write, telling my brother I'd never have the discipline to do it. On the rare occasions we'd talk, his first question was always whether I had given away the horses yet — as if the work, the inconvenience, and the expense of taking care of them were good reasons to give them away — the way he had given us to his mother.

After a few years of this, I terminated all contact with him. Nothing I did was good enough, and I finally understood it never would be. Lloyd stayed in touch with him, but I didn't. I was done. And then all these years later came the phone call from the hospital informing me he was dying. He had died for me so long ago, I thought his actual death would barely register. I thought I might even feel glad. But as I stood over his bed looking at the pale face with the intense brown eyes, listening to him struggle for every breath, I felt heartbroken for his suffering, for all our missed chances, and for not being able to save him. He had always been a giant to me, his once-lanky six-foot-four-inch frame the least of it. His personality, his intellect, his humor: these were the elements that made him larger than life. I suppose, too, it was his absence, especially when I was a child, the enormous hope that he would come back and the enormous disappointment when he didn't. I was in my mid-thirties before I stopped being afraid of him. By then I had a kind of fuck-you anger. I think I even said it to him once: *Fuck you!* That might have been the last time we talked. Now he was here, and for the first time in his life, he needed me.

A nurse approached. *Your sister Cindy is here to see him,* she said. *Only two family members are allowed at a time.*

I don't have a sister, I replied.

The nurse cocked her head and squinted at me. *Several young women have been here already,* she said, *all saying they were his daughters. I thought you were sisters.*

I'm his only daughter, I repeated, beginning to feel slightly sick, *and this is his only son.* Then I looked at my father. *Do you know who these women are?*

He nodded.

Do you want to see them?

He shook his head.

He has only two children, I said one more time. I wasn't sure whom I was protecting from these women, my father or myself. I had no idea who they were or in what capacity my father had known them, but it felt too creepy to ask. I didn't want to know. Later, when we went through his things, we discovered club memberships, tennis lessons, and charge accounts at department stores, all set up for women in their early twenties — we found boxes of photographs of them posed in and around my father's house. There was nothing overtly sexual — they were all dressed in casual clothes, but in every one of them, lips seemed too pouty or the profile of breasts too dominant — but they embarrassed my brother and me, and we closed the box and never looked at them again. My father's friendships with young women had been going on for years. There were five or six of them in particular, and when we called to find out what his relationship with them had been, they hung up.

I don't know why I found this so disturbing. Old men lusting after young women was nothing new. In the end, I think what bothered me had less to do with the sexual part and more to do with the relationship part. He had done for these women what he had never done for me. He had indulged them. He had paid for a tennis lesson, bought them a dress, or taken them to a nice restaurant — things a father might do for his daughter but that my father had never done for me. It was impossible not to wonder *why* all over again. It was impossible not to feel the totality of his rejection.

We were allowed to stay in the intensive care unit for

only thirty minutes, so Lloyd and I drove to the beach to walk his giant schnauzer, Eiger. It was gray and cold as we hunched our shoulders into our parkas, watching Eiger's graceful canter down the deserted beach. Even though we hadn't grown up together and lived too far apart to visit more than once or twice a year, at moments like this we shared an intimacy that made talking almost unnecessary. Neither one of us needed to say we wished we'd known him better or that we wished he'd known us. Neither one of us needed to say we felt like small children again, losing a last chance at something.

Later we were shocked when we walked into the mess and filth of his house. Because of emphysema, he'd been in a wheelchair for the previous ten years. Still, he'd had a private nurse seven days a week and a cleaning woman once a week, so we were unprepared for the level of neglect we saw everywhere. It was so depressing, I turned around and walked out, unsure I could stomach whatever we might find in the chaos. Even his front lawn was a ruin, scattered with rusting cars that hadn't been driven in years, the grass and shrubbery a wild, overgrown tangle. How had the neighbors allowed this? Why hadn't someone told us?

My brother didn't want to go through the house alone, so I relented and went back inside with him. We were looking for my father's false teeth, lost in the rush of loading him into the ambulance the day before. We wandered from room to room, almost too shocked to speak, noticing the stench and stains of cigarette smoke everywhere — in the walls, the furniture, fogging the windows. I saw some of my grandmother's art: paintings and ivory and jade, all broken and dusty, stained dark by smoke. Her collection of coffee-table-size art books, dozens of them, were stacked in sliding towers, stained with dark coffee-mug circles and yellowed with smoke, some still supporting containers of takeout food, half full with rotting meals. It was beyond belief that someone would live like this, someone with money, someone we knew.

The more we saw, the worse it became. There were expensive and beautiful things everywhere, ruined, broken, stained, and forgotten. Cameras, telescopes, televisions, books, artworks, tapestries, furniture, clothes. Not a single thing had escaped his neglect. The destruction was so complete, it almost seemed deliberate. It was impossible not to consider that I was related to a man who had done this, that I was his closest kin, that somehow this wreckage was a reflection of me.

I wondered, if I hadn't stopped smoking and drinking, is this what my life would have looked like? The word that kept coming to mind was *waste*. He had wasted most of the things in this house the same way he had wasted so much of his life. I thought about my life since I had stopped drinking—the horses, my friends, the job I loved, and the pretty little house with everything tucked in its place. But I knew enough about alcoholism to realize that if I didn't remain vigilant, I could end up just like my father—living alone in filth and chaos, paying strangers to "visit." I had the same beast inside me that my father had in him, but I never wanted to know the full extent of its power. It had controlled my life once for long enough. I never wanted to let it back in.

I hadn't always felt that way. Once I had admired his rebellious streak. For most of my childhood, I adored him for one simple reason—he wasn't afraid of his mother.

He drank and smoked and cursed, and more than once he had shocked her into speechlessness. In the epic struggle between a recalcitrant teenager and an overbearing mother, the teenager had won. She had dropped him off at boarding school, telling the headmaster of Choate that she wanted nothing more to do with him. They were as mismatched as a mother and son could be, and even years later, after he came back from the war and got married and my brother and I were in the picture, nothing much had changed. My grandmother still thought he was impossible (he was), and he still thought she was despotic (she was). Until my early twenties, I had glorified the impossible one. It hadn't mattered that I almost never saw him; the myth of him was enough. He was the one, the *only* one, I had ever seen stand up to Grandmother Richards.

Lloyd and I looked in all the places a set of false teeth could be and found everything but the teeth. Lloyd discovered a large sum of cash in the middle of a stack of old newspapers. I found a letter I had written to my father in the 1970s when I was living in Boston. It told him how much I loved teaching, how good my life was. Neither was true, but the letter was convincing. I had signed it *Love always*. That hadn't been true either. Not always. I found four or five address books, and — I couldn't help it — each time I'd look to see if Lloyd and I were listed. We never were. Not in a single one.

We gave up on the teeth and cleared off the clutter on the kitchen table so we could sit down and talk about what to do if our father died. He had no will and had never made his wishes about death or dying known to us. He wasn't religious, so we didn't even have church doctrine to help guide us. And then we talked about something that had bothered both of us for as long as we could remember. We had no idea where our mother was buried. Over the years, we had asked everyone in the family about it, including our father, but no one knew. It seemed incredible that such a thing could have slipped everyone's notice. At one point we found out from her sister that our mother's ashes had remained unclaimed in the funeral home for eight years before our mother's mother remembered to get them. Everyone thought someone else had taken care of it. To me it was one of the most egregious examples of how alcoholism can affect a family.

If we knew where our mother was buried, we reasoned, we could ask our father if he wanted to be with her. She was one of only two people he had loved for sure. The other one was his last wife, Betsy, whom he had divorced ten years earlier but with whom he had remained friends. We decided that at some point we would have to talk with our father about his wishes and about writing a will. Meanwhile, Lloyd would try one more time to find out where our mother was buried.

Within a few days, our father was transferred to a regular hospital room. He remained intubated, but his medical problems were no longer considered acute. Doctors couldn't tell us how much longer he might live. Emphysema can be a slow killer, little by little drowning the sufferer in his own fluids. I had to go back to work, but every Friday night, Lloyd and I met at the hospital and stayed with our father until Sunday night. I'd sit next to the bed and hold his hand while my brother went in and out of the room, using the pay phone down the hall to take care of my father's calculator business with the help of my father's accountant. He was also still trying to find our mother, calling my grandmother's old law firm, family members, and others who might have some idea of where she could be.

One day when a nurse came in to take blood from my father, for the first time it occurred to me that this was a pointless exercise, pointless and painful, as it was becoming harder to find a vein on my father's arms.

Stop, I said as I watched my father grimace every time the needle's point failed to find a vein.

The nurse looked annoyed and paused long enough to say, *Doctor's orders,* before she resumed the probing.

I mean it, I said and put my hand on her arm to stop her. It was the first time I understood that if I didn't object, nurses and doctors would continue pricking and prodding and running useless tests until he drew his last breath. Everything they did to him hurt him, and I wanted it to stop. They were not going to save his life or even prolong it. They were just going to continue to run tests because that's what hospitals did. I wish I had realized this sooner. I asked them to stop all tests. They made me sign a waiver, and after that, for the first time, I felt that I was really taking care of my father. The only procedures I allowed were those that made him more comfortable and his breathing less labored.

Taking care of my father was a lot like taking care of Georgia when she had been sick. Neither one of them could talk, so it was up to me to figure out when they needed something and what it was. With Georgia, it was how to manage her chronic pain, always a balancing act between undermedicating and increasing her discomfort and overmedicating and possibly causing her colic. It was also important to consider her state of mind. If she was confined for too long, she'd become "depressed" — there's no other word for this in the animal world, but the symptoms are similar to depressed humans: loss of appetite, loss of interest in their surroundings, and a lack of expressiveness. I always let Georgia know I knew where her pain was by running my hands down her legs and letting them rest on her hooves while I made little sympathetic noises in my throat. It helped her trust me enough so that when I had to ask her to do something difficult like lifting a foot, she'd make the effort because she knew I knew where the pain was.

Besides effective medication, the best treatment protocol for a sick horse is attention. Georgia loved being groomed when she was sick, and I'd think of projects to do in her stall or within sight of her stall so I could be with her for as long as possible. I brought a radio to the barn and tuned it to NPR so she could listen to the soothing sounds of classical music every morning. Hotshot and Tempo never grazed out of sight when she was sick, but I felt that my presence was just as important to her as theirs was. For that reason, whenever she was sick, I kept the light on in my kitchen all night (she could see the kitchen window from her stall) as a reminder to her that I wasn't far away.

Remembering how I had cared for Georgia helped me to care for my father, and a lot of the fears I had about taking care of him disappeared. One day, as I was sitting by his bed holding his hand, I felt all the anger toward him I'd carried for years leave my body. It was like exhaling a poison I'd inhaled a long time ago, and it had finally come out. In its place I felt an overwhelming sense of love for this terribly flawed father, this human being who had suffered greatly for most of his life. I saw how pointless and self-serving my anger had been, how rigid and self-righteous. I saw how it had stunted my own growth and had kept me from pursuing a relationship with him on more honest terms, terms that would have taken into account who he was rather than who I had wanted him to be.

For the first time, I told him I loved him. I knew that the way he nodded meant that he loved me, too. I was grateful there was time to have this experience with him, to feel the weight of my anger vanish and have it replaced with a new understanding. I wish it could have happened for my brother, but it didn't. Lloyd and my father continued to watch each other with a heartbreaking wariness. I couldn't make it go away. I couldn't fix whatever it was that kept them apart. For that reason Lloyd and I decided I was the one who should talk to our father about his wishes for burial and whether he wanted to write a will.

We started with the will. It seemed easier than asking him what he wanted done with his remains. My brother was a lawyer, so he would be in the room to help write it, but we also asked the private nurse who'd been with my father for years to be there, along with my father's doctor, whom he'd also known for years. Lloyd and I didn't want it to look like we were pressuring our father, not even to write a will if he didn't want to.

When we were all there, I sat on his bed and held his hand. In my other hand I held what I thought was his most up-to-date address book. If he wanted, I'd go through each entry to see if he wished to bequeath anything to that individual. Since my father couldn't talk, there was no other way to do it. He'd become so weak, his handwriting was no longer legible. I'd already gone through the book once on my own and had recognized only a few of the names. I had no idea who was a friend or a business associate.

We began. I asked him if he wanted to leave a will, and he nodded. I told him I'd brought his nurse and doctor into the room with us so he would have witnesses who could make sure that his wishes were recorded accurately. Then I held up his address book. Where did he want to begin? He waved the address book away and pointed at Lloyd and me.

You want to leave everything to us? Somehow this felt wrong. Even though we were his children, we barely knew him. We'd never really been part of his life. But he nodded vigorously. Just Lloyd and me. Suddenly this felt horribly awkward. It wasn't what I had expected. His nurse of many years was sitting in a chair across the room, a nurse I had always thought he was fond of. What about her? There was nothing to do but to ask.

Daddy, I said gently, *what about Mrs. Fielding?*

There was no hesitation. He shook his head. I couldn't look at Mrs. Fielding. I couldn't look at anyone. It suddenly seemed that Lloyd and I were the last people in the world who should be doing this. I tried one more time, holding up the address book.

You must have people you care about. If they aren't in here, you can still tell me. I can help you spell out their names. We can find them.

He closed his eyes and shook his head. As far as he was concerned, he was done. The will was written. Lloyd and I were the sole beneficiaries.

I still couldn't believe it, so I tried one more time. *What about Betsy?* I said. I knew he had loved his last wife. He still loved her. Everyone in our family had loved her. She was one of the best things that had happened to him.

He opened his eyes and turned to look at me. He nodded.

I started at ten thousand dollars. *Ten, twenty, thirty, forty, fifty.* He stopped me at fifty thousand. It seemed generous and right. She had done so much for him, for us. For almost ten years, she had given us a sense of what it was to have a family. We would gather at their house in Darien for Thanksgiving or Christmas, and it was Betsy who made us feel welcome. It was Betsy who gave us our first "traditions." When she told me they were going to separate, I had sobbed.

After the will was finished, weeks went by before I had the courage to bring up the subject of how and where my father wanted to be buried. But I could see that he was failing. I didn't have forever. One Saturday, as I was sitting with him, Lloyd came to the doorway and waved for me to come into the hall. He had found out where our mother was buried. She was in the graveyard of an Episcopal church in Saint James, Long Island, buried with other members of her family dating all the way back to 1863. We were so excited, we decided to go to the cemetery right then and there. We couldn't quite believe we'd found her, and we wanted to be sure. We'd have to see the graveyard with our own eyes.

I told our father that I thought we'd found where our mother was buried and that we wanted to see if it was true. He nodded that he understood. It was then that I asked him if it was indeed her gravesite, did he want to join her there when his time came? He nodded.

It was a two-hour drive to Saint James. On the way there we talked about our father dying and finding our mother's grave at the same time. It seemed so strange to us, this odd timing. We didn't talk about the way Lloyd and Daddy still weren't connecting, the hostile glances Lloyd received whenever he came into Daddy's hospital room. I didn't understand it; I never had. I was afraid it wasn't going to change, that Daddy would die and Lloyd would have to live with this hurt for the rest of his life. It seemed cruel and unnecessary. But I couldn't talk to my father about it either. He was too sick. And even if he hadn't been, he wouldn't have been able to articulate his feelings. I don't think he was even aware of how he acted toward Lloyd. Unlike me, there was nothing Lloyd had ever done to earn this hostility. It had just been there forever, a kind of emotional infanticide.

We arrived in Saint James in the late afternoon; it was a small, picturesque town at the edge of Long Island Sound with colonial houses and split-rail fences. I didn't know why our mother would be buried there, what her family's connection was to Saint James. We found the only Episcopal church in town, a small stone structure with a cemetery in the back designated as a national historic site.

We entered the church through the front door and immediately bumped into a tall man wearing a dark suit, who introduced himself as the minister. When we told him why we were there, he escorted us into a small office that contained the records of every burial going back to the 1700s. We weren't sure of the year of our mother's burial, but we estimated it to be about eight years after her death, sometime around 1962. It didn't take long. Within a few minutes, we found her name in a burial logbook:

Marguerite Devereux Richards. It told us the date she had been buried and where the plot was.

It was a cold gray day in mid-March. Lloyd and I shivered our way across the small cemetery, looking for the large flat stone that would bear the name of our great-great-grandmother Antoinette Huntington Devereux Andrews. We actually remembered visiting her penthouse apartment at the top of the Garden City Hotel. I must have been about four or five years old. She was bedridden by then, but she always greeted us with a friendly smile and offered us candy, which she kept in a drawer next to her bed. But it was her chauffeur, Charles, whom we liked the most. After a brief visit with our great-great-grandmother, we would go with Charles to his apartment in the basement of the building and play with his bird, a crow he called Crow. After we had petted Crow and eaten more treats, Charles would tuck us into a fur throw in the back seat of our great-great-grandmother's Bentley and drive us back to Rye. It had never occurred to us that she was rich.

The minister had already told us we wouldn't find our mother's name engraved on the stone. After her ashes had been buried, he said, no one had added her name. The cemetery was so small, it was easy to look at every stone, to read every name. And just like that, after years of not knowing where she was, we had found her. We also found her mother, Marguerite Devereux Harrison, buried in 1984. So there, before us, were four generations of Devereux women. Where were the men? The sons and grandsons? We had no idea.

Before we left, we asked the minister for permission to bury our father there. We didn't know if this would be allowed, if historic sites were restricted or forbidden. But he said that because this was a family plot and as long as our father was cremated, it would be fine. He could be buried with his wife and in-laws. I didn't remember my father saying anything very nice about his mother-in-law, someone with whom he would soon be sharing eternity. She had been an alcoholic, and my father had once described her as spoiled and bored. I had never known her well enough to form my own opinion of her. Certainly, she was rich. She seemed to travel perpetually, going back and forth between her homes in Switzerland and Maine, as well as spending a lot of time in Bermuda and the American Southwest. She liked to paint in oils. She had never taken an interest in Lloyd or me. That was all I knew about her.

I wondered, too, how my mother would have felt about having her husband of eight years buried next to her. The family joke was that she had died to get away from him, since divorce wasn't an option. But I didn't know if that was true. Still, it was hard to imagine she could have been happy because it was hard to imagine how anyone could have been happy living with our father. He was already an alcoholic in their early married life. His behavior had always been over the top, in good and bad ways, but living with the bad would have made living with the good difficult. He was funny and smart and charming, but how could that negate the anger, the irresponsibility, and the drunk falls that led to job losses over and over again?

Lloyd and I discussed this on the way back to the hospital. Would burying our father next to our mother disturb her everlasting peace? Were we doing this more for ourselves, without considering what her wishes might have been? Lloyd had many more memories of our parents together than I did, and he was able to recall some genuinely pleasant moments of all of us being together, mostly at the beach, a place both our parents had loved. He also remembered our parents playing tennis together, going off to cocktail parties dressed to the nines, and looking happy. He remembered them laughing. That was enough for me. Whatever bad feelings had existed between them, surely in death they no longer mattered. They had loved each other once, and whatever beliefs our father had about death, the thought of being near our mother again seemed to comfort him now.

It was late Sunday night when we returned to the hospital, past nine o'clock, and I wasn't sure if we should disturb our father with the news about finding the gravesite. We decided to peek in his room, and if he was awake, we would tell him; if he wasn't, we'd save the news for the next weekend. Both of us had to work the next day and had long drives ahead of us. But as soon as he saw us, he waved us into the room. He was sitting up because he was always sitting up; he couldn't breathe any other way. Lloyd sat on one side of the bed and I on the other.

We found the grave, I told him. *We found Mom.* I told him where it was and who else was buried there. I told him how pretty it was, how peaceful. *Anyone buried there has to be cremated,* I explained.

He nodded that he understood and that cremation was OK. He seemed relieved that the issue of where our mother was buried had been resolved. Or maybe it was the resolution of his own burial plans that gave him some peace. At any rate, he seemed more relaxed to me, less hostile to Lloyd, who was sitting close to him.

By the time we left the hospital, it was so late that Lloyd decided he would follow me to my house, spend the night there, and then leave early the next day for the five-hour drive to northern Vermont. He'd miss a day of work, but he was too tired to make it all the way home.

By the time we had driven back, eaten, and taken care of the horses, it was after 2 A.M., when we said good night. I must have fallen asleep right away because at 2:20 the phone rang, startling me awake. It was the doctor calling from the hospital to tell us our father had just died.

Lloyd was in the downstairs guest room, but the house was so small, I knew he'd be able to hear me, so I didn't even get out of bed. *Daddy just died,* I called out to him.

Oh, God, he answered.

And that was it. We were too tired to get up and talk about it. It didn't really register. I went right back to sleep. It wasn't until the next day, in the middle of a staff meeting, that I suddenly burst into tears and had to leave the room. Later my boss came to my office and suggested that I take the rest of the week off to make whatever arrangements I needed to make for my father.

I didn't really know him, I said, embarrassed that I couldn't stop crying.

I arranged for Tempo's owner, Judy, to take care of the horses, Pilly, and Bosco, and I drove back to my father's house in Connecticut. My brother was already there, standing in the middle of the living room, looking at the mess everywhere. It struck me as a sad but fitting summation of our father's life: a big mess. It had had all the potential to be otherwise, but he couldn't do it. He couldn't overcome his own demons. It made me horribly sad. I walked through every room, and it was the same: chaos and destruction. Attached to the house was a warehouse full of electronic calculators and anything else that had caught my father's eye. It was like walking into Best Buy, the Sharper Image, and Neiman Marcus all rolled into one. Stuff was piled on shelves all the way to the ceiling, a lot of it brand-new, a lot of it sticky or stained with spilled Coke or coffee.

I felt overwhelmed. Lloyd and I had to deal with this — his clothes, the furniture, the art, hundreds of calculators, the rusty cars on the front lawn. All of it. Somehow we had to empty this house and have it cleaned. We had to figure out whom to call, whom and what to pay, and how and when to honor his life. All for a man we hardly knew. When Lloyd left for the hospital to get the death certificate, I sat at the kitchen table and cried. I missed my father. I missed the fact that I never really had one, and I mourned that now I never would. It all seemed horribly wrong, for him, for us, for anyone who knew him. He had been out of reach to all of us, a blinding light that had burned itself out over and over again.

I knew I couldn't go through his house. I couldn't look at and touch his things and decide what to do with them. It was too painful. I called a good friend, a man I had worked with at a former job who I knew had stamina and great organizational skills, and asked him if he could help my brother go through the house. He said he'd come right away and stay through the weekend if we needed him. When Lloyd returned from the hospital, we went to the funeral home together to pick up the ashes. We chose a red marble urn, perfect for a man who loved red so much he had once asked the gardener to plant only red flowers.

His cars were red, his boats, his dishes, and a lot of his clothes. Now he would be ensconced in red forever. It was the first thing my brother and I were able to smile about.

When we returned to the house, my friend Phil was there waiting for us. I felt guilty leaving my brother and Phil to do everything, but I knew I couldn't do it. I couldn't even go back inside the house. My brother understood and wasn't angry. He seemed energized by the task ahead, ready to work through whatever he was feeling by doing hard labor.

I took the urn with my father's ashes and headed back to Olivebridge. When I arrived, I put the urn on the dining room table because it faced the pond, the pastures, and the mountains beyond. My father would have liked the view. He especially would have liked my red dining room chairs. I kept him on the table for weeks, introducing him to friends whenever they came over, mentioning to some that my father had never been so polite, so easy to entertain, as he was now in his urn. I talked to him whenever I was home. I told him he was a lousy father but I loved him anyway. I always had.

My brother and I planned a memorial service, to be held in May at the Episcopal church in Saint James. We wanted it to be later in the spring because some of my father's oldest friends would be there, men he had served with in World War II, and we didn't want them to have to deal with snow and ice. My father had been a bomber pilot and was the first of the six men he had flown with to die. They had stayed in touch with one another all these years, sharing memories of something the rest of us couldn't even imagine. My father was closer to them than to anyone in his family. In many ways, I felt this service was for them.

Photographs of the memorial service show a sunny day with a lot of people milling around on the bright green grass of early spring. In the background is the stone church, and beyond that, the historic graveyard. My aunts and uncles are talking and smiling at one another. My brother is sweeping my cousin Laura into his arms, and she is laughing and holding down the hem of her skirt. Phil is there, helping my brother's three children collect caterpillars and letting them crawl across the enormous flat stone marking our family's plot. Betsy is there with her best friend, Gayla. They are mugging into the camera because they have just lost a lot of weight and are showing off their newly svelte figures. My father's bomber squadron is there, five aging veterans laughing into the sunshine about something my father once did, something about carrying a ham across the desert in Tunisia, something about illegal whiskey. I am there, smiling at cousins I haven't seen in twenty years, catching up on who lives where and what they do.

What the camera didn't show was how liberated I felt. It was as though a heavy weight had lifted, and I could take a deep breath for the first time in my life. I had been unaware of how much my father's criticism had dogged me. Whether he was present or not, his voice was always there, just over my shoulder, often paralyzing me with doubts and fears. Only with his death did I realize how pervasive this was and the extent to which I had allowed myself to be undermined. My grandmother's voice had often mingled with his, and together, the chorus of criticism was deafening.

The day after my father's memorial, I rode Georgia at the edge of my neighbor's field. It was one of those spring mornings in May that seemed like a miracle of sun and warmth after a long cold winter. Pilly trotted across the field ahead of us, and killdeer flew low above the pasture, their cries piercing the morning air like fresh ideas. Everything felt new because it *was* new. It was spring, and we were starting over, I and every other living being, on the dawn of this magnificent day.

The sense of freedom that followed my father's death seemed to deepen with every passing week. I could be myself, *really* be myself, and no one would mind, at least no one who mattered. It was an incredible feeling, a sense that no one was watching, as though the security cameras had been turned off and I could come and go unmonitored. I could do anything, and it would never get back to "headquarters." More and more I let myself entertain notions, silly ideas about the ways I wanted to spend my time, the ways I wanted to live. I'd ask myself while I was riding Georgia, *Is your life as you imagined it? Is there something else you want to do? Is there something missing?*

I came up with a lot of answers about what was missing: inner peace, confidence, and audacity (this almost seemed like a luxury, but I thought it was an important part of smart risk-taking; also, Georgia was audacious and I'd always loved that about her). The list went on and on. Some of the things on it were silly, like trying to figure out how to wrap my leg around my head in yoga. But one that made the list over and over again was writing. I wanted to write. I didn't know what I wanted to write; I only knew I had an overwhelming desire to put pencil to paper and write something. Anything. If you've ever imagined writing a novel, you know how trying to come up with an idea can shut you down fast. Just the word *novel* is enough to scare an aspiring writer. Not only did it have to be a good story, but it had to be Tolstoyian in its scope of social, political, and philosophical profundity. It had to be important. Something worth spending five years of your life on while you are sitting in a darkened room chewing your nails to the quick. Or did it?

Sad though I was about my father's death, the freedom that came with it was a gift I hadn't imagined. And as I rode Georgia that morning in the soft light of May, I knew I was about to use that gift to do the one thing I'd been more afraid of doing than anything else. I knew I was about to sit down and write.

{CHAPTER 11}

I SAT IN FRONT of the open wood stove in my living room, wrapped in the smell of burning logs. The downstairs lights were turned low, and the house felt warm and cozy and clean. My Siamese cat, Bosco, was curled on my lap, purring his contentment, his fur hot to the touch. Pilly was on the floor next to us, asleep in her doughnut bed, which was pulled close to the fire. I looked around the house; almost ten years after buying it, I still couldn't believe it was mine. The first time I saw it, I felt it would be a healing house, though I hadn't known how or why. It was late December, but there was no snow on the ground, so you could see the "bones" of the place, as the realtor had said—the stone walls, the open pastureland with the pond at the center, and on a small rise, the red glass house flooded with sun. The sight of it had quickened my heart, and before I even walked through the front door I knew I was home.

As I followed the realtor from room to room in the empty house, the notion that I could heal played on a continuous loop in my head, though I wasn't sure what it referred to specifically. My alcoholism? The trauma of a bad marriage, a bad childhood, a lost horse? Foremost on my mind that day was how sick I was from drinking the night before, followed by how sick I was that I didn't have Georgia to graze in the perfect pastures. But the feeling that I would heal persisted as we climbed the spiral stairs to the master bedroom, with its view of hay fields stretching to the woods and the Catskill Mountains beyond. *This is a healing house,* insisted the voice.

A few days later I moved in, but I was still drinking and still didn't have my horse, and I felt as sick as ever. If this was a healing house, what did it mean and when would the healing start? I staggered up the spiral stairs drunk one night, gripping the rail so I wouldn't fall and break my neck alone in my new house. When I reached the top, I went outside to the balcony and stood there shivering and despondent in the frigid January air because there I was, starting my life over, only nothing had changed—I was still drinking and Georgia was still gone.

I had left my husband and moved to a place where I didn't know a single soul—a place where no one knew about the old me, the one who drank and slurred her words on the phone at night and later hid in the barn from an angry man. I moved to a place where no one knew I had lost a house and a horse and the childhood dream of living on a farm in the Adirondacks. I moved to a place where the old me could be dreamed up like a good book, so even my past could look as shiny and bright as the new me who had moved to Olivebridge.

Instead, I drank more than ever and cried about my bad luck and told my lawyer, *I don't give a crap about the money, just get the horse.* Each time, I drove to a different liquor store to buy my wine so that no one in the new rural community, where everyone knew everyone, would notice that the young woman who had just bought the old Stock place had a problem with booze. I might have killed myself while driving drunk or falling down the spiral stairs or drowning in the pond as I staggered around the land I had just bought and loved so much. I might have died from choking on my own vomit or falling off the balcony to the driveway below or in one of a dozen other ways in which people who stumble around blind, drunk, and crazy often die.

Before I could figure out how to save myself, an angel had appeared in the form of an old friend who came to visit from Boston and suggested we stop drinking together. I humored her and said OK, and just like that — *just like that* — the nightmare began to end. It was April 23, and no date, not even my own birthday, will ever seem as important to me as the day I stopped drinking.

Ten years later, at forty-three, I was without a cigarette, a drink, or the wrong man, and my beloved Morgan mare grazed outside the kitchen window in the pasture with her two equine siblings. My life was full of calm, if not peace, and in many ways fulfilled the childhood dream of living in a sunny house on a farm surrounded by dogs and horses. In fact, the dream had manifested itself so perfectly in terms of the house, the land, the animals, the career, and the community of friends I had found, it sometimes felt as though I had fallen into it from nowhere, that no effort had been involved, but rather, in my incoherent stumblings through the wreckage of my former life, I had simply bumped into the new one and grabbed hold. It seemed impossible that, in fact, step by deliberate step over the course of many years, I had slowly crawled out of some dark pit by way of my own two feet — six if you counted Georgia's, which I surely did.

I was surprised I had the guts. So many times along the way I wanted to give up and walk out, the big kind of walkout where you never come back because your heart has stopped beating. The two words that best described how it felt to be sober the first few years were *overwhelmed* and *fearful*. As I emerged from the walking coma that is alcoholism, I felt as though I'd stepped into a world that had left me behind in every way, with no possibility of catching up. Catching up would have meant overcoming the impossible — a stifling shyness kept in place by the belief that I was fundamentally and permanently a grossly inadequate human being.

But AA taught me that such a belief was not only absurd but also a kind of arrogance used to perpetuate the myth that I was a victim and therefore bore no responsibility for how my life unfolded. It was a shock to learn that no one was going to join me on the pity pot, but if I was willing to get off, I'd have a platoon behind me if I wanted it. I became more than just sober in AA. I became human. Not subhuman, not superhuman — alcoholics have a hard time with moderation of any kind — but just human enough to take the lid off and free whatever potential existed.

I didn't kill myself because I didn't think anyone else could take care of Georgia. Not the way I did. Some days it was that simple. It was enough to keep me not just sober but alive until whatever the insurmountable problem of the day was had passed. Often the problem was financial worries and the fear that I would lose the house. Sometimes it was something hurtful a friend or a client said, a criticism that reopened one festering wound or another. There were so many wounds in the early days, they were easy to find. Anything that felt like rejection was the most tender. Once I wrung my hands for a week over not being invited to a certain birthday party. Another time it seemed easier to end my life than to face the possibility that my beloved neighbor, Henry, might not speak to me for the rest of his life because one year I stopped buying hay from him. My back problems had become so bad, I could no longer drive my truck onto his fields and pick up my own hay and stack it in my hayloft, and Henry was too old to do it for me. I had no choice but to buy my hay from someone who could deliver and stack it. Henry took it personally. He didn't speak to me for two years, and although it felt awful, I learned patience and to leave alone something over which I had no control.

But my biggest fear, especially as the years passed and I'd been sober for a while, was that I would die without once knowing what it was like to be loved. I'd had my share of relationships, but never a sane, sober, and mature one and never one that hadn't felt clingy. I had no single women friends, and it was easy to feel there was something wrong with the fact that I'd been unable to connect deeply with someone from my own species. I wasn't connected, not in the way that Georgia and Tempo and Hotshot were, not even in the way my geese were, who never strayed more than a few feet from each other. Watching my friends with their families, looking at my herd, and seeing my geese spend the day together on the pond, I became aware of how lonely I often felt.

When I saw bad relationships — and there were plenty of them — I was glad I wasn't connected, and I was glad I'd escaped the bad connections of my own making. That was the good part about living alone — the absence of a bad connection. If you'd ever had one, living alone could feel pretty good, and that's how I felt most of the time about living alone — *pretty* good.

But inevitably the loneliness returned. I dealt with it by spending time with my horses and dog, seeing friends, and working long hours at the rehab. I dealt with it by staying busy, too busy, exhausting myself enough so I was too tired to notice how my loneliness seemed to be increasing.

In the previous few months I'd been going to the barn at night to check on Georgia. She had foundered again in the late fall, and now, seven months later in March, she was just beginning to come out of it. This time the damage was permanent. Her coffin bone had rotated and descended too far, and I would never be able to ride her again. I didn't mind. My back had all but grounded me, but I worried that Georgia would feel pasture-bound and bored. I worried what her lameness would do to her status in the herd. It was terrible to watch a herd's bold and bossy mare — its character and sometimes clown — be cowed by illness. For months Georgia had been restricted to the small outdoor pen attached to her stall. Hotshot and Tempo, though free to roam, had always foraged near her, never more than a few yards from her fence. I'd scatter hay next to the outside of her pen, and even if the wind blew it farther away, they wouldn't leave her.

Now, with her front hooves wrapped in layers of gauze and duct tape and then squeezed into bright blue padded sneakers, she was walking around again pretty well. I'd let her out of her pen, and she was free to go anywhere in either pasture, but her illness had taken away some of her confidence. I could tell by the way she didn't drive Hotshot away from the watering trough and by the way she let him eat his hay in peace. She was no longer micromanaging his life. She was no longer micromanaging mine. I could walk around her without being frisked for treats, and I could visit with the other two without her chasing them away.

It was such a big personality change, it made me feel protective of her. I had the urge to check on her in the middle of a winter night to see if she was OK. I lifted the sleeping cat off my lap and resettled him in the warm chair. It was after eleven, and the big round thermometer nailed to the cedar tree off the back deck said it was twenty degrees. I opened the basement door and started pulling barn clothes off the hooks on the wall — an old red down parka, the insulated navy blue warm-up pants, a hat, and gloves. Pilly lifted her head and watched me get into the clothes she knew meant I was going to the barn. I could see her debating whether to give up her warm place by the fire for a cold walk to a cold barn. In the end, her sense of adventure won and she struggled to her feet, still limping from her broken leg. I grabbed a bag of carrots from the refrigerator and gave one to Pilly, who always carried it across the pasture and ate it lying down in the center aisle of the barn while the horses ate their grain.

She carried her carrot across the dark, frozen pasture with only half a moon and a few stars to light our way. I knew the horses would be inside, eating what was left of the hay I had scattered around their stalls five hours earlier. It was a cold night, and Georgia and Tempo might be huddled together in Tempo's stall, with Hotshot standing nearby in the aisle just outside Georgia's reach. They all had thick woolly coats, and the barn was well protected from the wind. I talked to Pilly as we walked across the pasture, wanting the horses to hear my voice so they wouldn't be afraid of the sound of footsteps crossing the frozen field in the dark. They always seemed alarmed by my late-night visits, no matter how often I came.

Just inside the barn, I felt around the wall for the light switch and flipped it on, and there they were, all crammed into Tempo's stall, blinking sleepy eyes into the sudden glare. It was the first time I'd ever seen all three of them in one stall. Georgia had never allowed it, and I wondered if her permitting it now was another sign of how her illness had changed her. One at a time, they left Tempo's stall and came to get the carrots they knew I had. They seemed sweet and vulnerable, slightly confused by the late-night visit and by Pilly, the new dog, who'd been coming with me to the barn for only a few weeks.

I put my hand through Georgia's halter and walked her up and down the center aisle just to see how she walked, how much her limp might have improved or worsened since I last tested her a few hours earlier. As we walked, I took off my glove and stroked her shoulder, telling her how well she was doing, how pleased I was to see her feeling better. I loved being near her, walking next to the warm, powerful neck that bobbed up and down with each step, her profile a study in Morgan perfection. She let me cup her face in my hands, kiss her nose, and tease her icy whiskers with my fingers. Hotshot and Tempo returned to Tempo's stall and watched us going up and down the aisle. I wondered if they knew what we were doing, if any of them connected my presence to Georgia's illness. How much did horses understand about the things we did with them and to them?

I didn't know the answer to that question, but I was sure Georgia knew I loved her. I knew she felt a connection. She never expressed her affection toward me in grand gestures — not like mine toward her, which she tolerated because maybe she knew I couldn't help them. Mostly I knew she cared about me because she was so proprietary. I was like her stall; unless you were invited in, you'd have to be crazy to step across the threshold. The other horses knew not to come near us when Georgia and I were together. I was her human, the rag doll she dragged around the house by the foot. Drug addicts might call it tough love, but with Georgia it was rough love.

After walking her up and down the aisle a few times, I decided her footing seemed OK; there was no need for pain medication because she wasn't limping or hesitating. Mostly she seemed eager to rejoin Hotshot and Tempo in Tempo's stall. She hated being left out; she hated not being the center of attention. I watched her walk into Tempo's stall and shove Hotshot aside so she could stand next to Tempo. Hotshot accepted his repositioning without objection. He never objected to anything she did, which was a good thing, or there would have been an ongoing battle.

When they had reshuffled themselves, I went back to the tack room and climbed the spiral stairs to the hayloft. I couldn't resist giving them a little more hay to munch on during the long, cold night. It was tricky to keep a horse at the right weight, especially older horses. Tempo and Hotshot needed more grain and hay to keep weight on, but Georgia needed almost nothing. I had to be careful with her, especially with her repeated founders. It was all connected for a horse — diet, weight, metabolism, and hoof health. In the spring and summer, when the grass was rich, I'd often put a muzzle on her after only an hour or two of grazing. More grazing than that was too much for her. She did better on a diet of mostly hay because it wasn't as rich.

The hayloft in my barn is one of my favorite places. There is nothing special about it except that it's a hayloft and it's mine; I can go there whenever I want. It holds about six hundred fifty bales when it's full, but by March it's half empty. I dropped a few leaves of hay through the hole in the loft ceiling above Tempo's stall, and right away I could see the horses reshuffling themselves to start eating. I watched for a minute to see if Georgia would kick Hotshot out of the stall, and if she did, I'd drop more hay into his stall so he wouldn't be left out. But she didn't, and I could hear the contented grinding of molars as each horse selected his or her favorite sweet grasses.

Afterward, I opened the double hayloft doors, the ones just below the peak of the roof where Lane's carved wooden horse hung — the memory of my dear friend inextricably bound to this barn. I sat in the doorway dangling my legs over the edge and looked toward the Shawangunk Ridge in the south and Henry's barn and fields to the west and thought what I always thought when I sat in this perch. How lucky I was to have found this haven, this home. How lucky I was that I hadn't lost it all to alcoholism.

My life so easily could have gone another way. I met people every day whose lives had, men and women who came to the rehab who'd been drinking or drugging for twenty years or longer, who'd lost everything: families, jobs, health. They'd arrive with everything they owned in a shopping bag, penniless, homeless, and friendless. That could have been me. That could have been my ending except for the love of a horse. For Georgia I had wanted to be a better person; for her I wanted to get well. I'd had ten years of therapy in the saddle — so many mornings in the company of my dog, my horse, and my demons, immersed in healing nature — on the trails through the woods of the Catskill Mountains. How lucky I'd been to love horses and luckier still to love Georgia.

I sat in my hayloft perch and realized that if I had to, I could go on living my life exactly the way it was, without a partner. Maybe I had other lessons to learn, and living with a partner was never going to be one of them. But I knew for sure I couldn't live without horses; I couldn't live without Georgia, Hotshot, and Tempo, whose care kept me grounded and sane and whose existence gave my life such a joyful purpose. I sat in my hayloft perch and said to myself what I always said to myself if I sat there long enough. Thank God. Thank God for horses and thank God for Georgia, who had taken one lost and frightened woman for the ride of her life.

ACKNOWLEDGMENTS

I'd like to say thank you to the dream team at Houghton Mifflin Harcourt, beginning with my editor, Jenna Johnson, who took an idea and helped me shape it into a book. Thank you, Jenna, for your guidance and patience. A big thank you to the rest of the team at HMH for their hard work on my behalf: Rachael Hoy, Dalia Geffen, Carla Gray, Michelle Bonanno, and Johnathan Wilber.

Thank you to my wonderful writing group who gave invaluable feedback along the way: Gretchen Primack, Abigail Thomas, Melissa Holbrook Pierson, Susan Krawitz, and Susan Sindall.

Once again, thanks to Helen Zimmermann, the best agent an author could have.

And thanks to my beloved Dennis, who makes everything better.